Teaching Poetry in a Digital World

Teaching Poetry in a Digital World supports English language arts (ELA) educators for grades 6–12 to incorporate digital literacy in their classrooms by teaching the reading and writing of poetry.

In an increasingly digital age, educators must adapt to meet the changing needs and interests of their students by incorporating technology into the classroom. This book introduces its audience to the e-Poetry Framework. This framework demonstrates how poetry might present itself in a literacy-based unit with the benefit of a technology medium to share with the world. Examples include teaching zip-ode poetry, incorporating haiku with the creation of GIFs, and ethically discussing AI with nonet poems. With adaptable lesson plans and assessments, as well as educator examples, the book will inspire teachers to create intentional student-centered e-Poetry units.

The book is aligned with ELA literacy standards, International Society for Technology in Education (ISTE) educator standards, and National Council of Teachers of English (NCTE)'s position statement for integrating technology into ELA classrooms. It is a key resource for secondary school educators teaching ELA, creative writing, and digital media.

Stefani Boutelier has over 20 years of teaching experience in K–20 and is currently an Associate Professor of Education at Aquinas College. She teaches pre-service and in-service teacher courses in instructional design, literacy, ed tech, and research methods as well as general education first-year seminar courses.

Sarah J. Donovan is an Associate Professor of Secondary Education English at Oklahoma State University and founder of Ethical ELA. Launched in 2015, the Ethical ELA website hosts a monthly five-day online poetry writing experience with teachers and Verselove, 30 days of poetry writing in celebration of National Poetry Month. Her work focuses on how writing poetry shapes learning and well-being.

Also Available from Routledge Eye On Education
(www.routledge.com/eyeoneducation)

Teaching Reading and Literature with Classroom Talk:
Dialogical Approaches and Practical Strategies in the
Secondary ELA Classroom
Dawan Coombs

Teach This Poem, Volume I: The Natural World
Madeleine Fuchs Holzer and The Academy of American Poets

Student-Centered Literacy Assessment
in the 6-12 Classroom: An Asset-Based Approach
Sean Ruday

Grammar Inquiries, Grades 6–12:
An Inquiry- and Asset-Based Approach
to Grammar Instruction
Sean Ruday

The Antiracist English Language Arts Classroom
Keisha Rembert

The Literacy Coaching Handbook:
Working With Teachers to Increase Student
Achievement, 2nd edition
Diana Sisson and Betsy Sisson

Teaching Poetry in a Digital World

Inspiring Poetry Writing through Technology in Grades 6–12

Stefani Boutelier and Sarah J. Donovan

Routledge
Taylor & Francis Group

NEW YORK AND LONDON

Designed cover image: © Getty Images.

First published 2025
by Routledge
605 Third Avenue, New York, NY 10158

and by Routledge
4 Park Square, Milton Park, Abingdon, Oxon, OX14 4RN

Routledge is an imprint of the Taylor & Francis Group, an informa business

© 2025 Stefani Boutelier and Sarah J. Donovan

The right of Stefani Boutelier and Sarah J. Donovan to be identified as authors of this work has been asserted in accordance with sections 77 and 78 of the Copyright, Designs and Patents Act 1988.

All rights reserved. No part of this book may be reprinted or reproduced or utilised in any form or by any electronic, mechanical, or other means, now known or hereafter invented, including photocopying and recording, or in any information storage or retrieval system, without permission in writing from the publishers.

Trademark notice: Product or corporate names may be trademarks or registered trademarks, and are used only for identification and explanation without intent to infringe.

ISBN: 978-1-032-94686-3 (hbk)
ISBN: 978-1-032-94684-9 (pbk)
ISBN: 978-1-003-58123-9 (ebk)

DOI: 10.4324/9781003581239

Typeset in Palatino
by KnowledgeWorks Global Ltd.

To the teachers who dare to bridge the timeless beauty of poetry with the boundless possibilities of technology. Your commitment to innovation and imagination breathes new life into words, empowering students to find their voices in a world that is ever-changing. This work is for you—those who light the way for the poets of tomorrow, one verse at a time.

Contents

Meet the Authors ix

PART I 1

1 Poetry in Our Digital World 3

2 Digital Citizenry for Content Creators 16

3 e-Poetry Framework: The Power of Choice
   in Digital Poetry Composition 36

4 From Draft to Digital: Understanding Writing
   Process Approaches to Poetry and Technology 55

PART II 71

5 Haiku in Motion: Celebrating School
   Community through GIF Poetry 73

6 Place-Based Poetry: Zip-Odes and
   YouTube Shorts 95

7 AI + Nonet: Machine and Human Poetry
   Collaboration 124

8 Echoes of Persuasion: Two-Voiced Spoken
   Word Recordings 151

9 Concrete Piles of Positivity with Templates 175

10 Playing with Words: Enhancing Poetry
Through Gamification 193

Epilogue: Embracing the e-Poetry Journey 205
Index. 209

Meet the Authors

Stefani Boutelier, PhD, is a scholar, educator, and advocate whose work bridges education, technology, and community development. She works collaboratively to improve pedagogical practices at the local, national, and international levels through a feminist andragogical lens. Dr. Boutelier is an Associate Professor of Education at Aquinas College in Michigan. In addition to that role, she is also the Graduate Research Program Director for the School of Education and the Coordinator of Instructional Technology for Academic Affairs. Dr. Boutelier teaches courses for pre-service and in-service educators on instructional design, engaging diverse learners, literacy, ed tech, and research methods. As well, she has also taught First Year Seminar, Communication, and Irish Studies courses.

Her K–12 teaching was in Southern California prior to moving into teacher preparation. During this time she taught various levels of secondary English language arts (ELA), Reading, AVID, Cultural Literature, and adult ESL courses. Her research endeavors started when she was teaching middle school as she pursued her PhD in Education from Chapman University in Orange, CA, through her dissertation, Translated Identity: Multilingual Reality of Tween Identity Formation. Dr. Boutelier has made contributions to the field of education in areas of digital literacy, innovative pedagogy, equitable assessment practices, and teacher preparation. Her work continues to explore critical relationships and identity to re-center the learners involved. You can find her work in peer-reviewed journals (e.g., *International Journal of Qualitative Methods* and *Journal of Technology and Teacher Education*), chapters in books (e.g., Revolutionizing English Education: AI in the Classroom), and educational blogs (e.g., Edutopia). As well, she is an original member of GAP (Gendered Academic Productivity)—an international, cross-departmental collective of academic researchers.

Stefani is an International Society for Technology in Education (ISTE) Certified educator and trainer. She is also a Google for Education Certified Trainer, Apple Teacher, Microsoft Innovative Educator, and an Adobe Creative Educator. She has collaborated with undergraduate and graduate students in publishing educational articles and presenting at conferences across the country. She has been invited to lead trainings around technology and design, partake on various boards, and consult with multiple groups aligned to technology, AI literacy, curricular design, andragogy, and youth violence prevention. Stefani is an experienced conference speaker and panelist with over 30 presentations earning multiple fellowships and grants to partake in these opportunities. As well, she also has creative publications in genres of poetry, short stories, and humor.

Her service is widespread from local to international organizations. She is currently serving a three-year term as a MACUL (Michigan Association of Computer Users for Learning) Board Member, is an active member of other education organizations (e.g., National Council of Teachers of English [NCTE], KETS), and is an associate member of The Educator Collaborative. In addition, her community advocacy spans from co-facilitating GET (Girls Empowering Together), mentoring for 7 years with exploited teens through Wedgwood Christian Services (WCS)/The Manasseh Project, Leading the MACUL Women's Forum, and volunteering to review many manuscripts and awards. She was awarded the WCS Molly Guillime Volunteer of the Year Award in 2020 and also was the community award winner for the Adobe+ISTE challenge in the same year. Dr. Boutelier's multifaceted career reflects a dedication to addressing the unique challenges and opportunities the intersections of technology present for learning. She loves to bring people together, make connections, and learn along the way.

Sarah J. Donovan, PhD, is a celebrated author and educator dedicated to reshaping secondary ELA through her roles as Associate Professor at Oklahoma State University and an active voice in poetry pedagogy, inclusive literacy, and youth literature. Her work centers on the power of literature and writing to build inclusive, humanizing spaces for students and teachers alike. Donovan is best known for her expertise in using poetry and young adult literature as tools for fostering community, nurturing identity, and enabling teachers and students to develop curriculum that reflects human experiences.

With a PhD in English from the University of Illinois, Chicago, Donovan's research introduced "Transactional Consciousness Theory," a framework for teaching complex topics like genocide through literature, helping students engage empathetically with difficult histories. She has since authored numerous academic and creative works, including articles in journals such as Research in Teaching English, English Education, Teaching/Writing and English Journal, and co-authored books and chapters on writing pedagogy, trauma literacy, and teacher identity. Her publications reflect her commitment to anti-bias, anti-racist (ABAR) practices and the importance of giving voice to marginalized narratives in education. She and Eliza Ramirez won the Linda Rief Award for their article in Voices from the Middle.

Beyond her publications, Donovan is deeply invested in mentorship and collaboration. She actively supports undergraduate and graduate students, as well as practicing teachers, in their research and creative endeavors.

Donovan's reach extends to her work with the NCTE and the Assembly on Literature for Adolescents (ALAN), where she has served as a board member and columnist. She has received national recognition for her impact on teaching youth literature. She frequently presents at conferences, addressing themes such as poetry's role in education, supporting LGBTQ+ students, and developing inclusive pedagogies that challenge biases. Her workshops and presentations emphasize the need for ethical, empathetic teaching practices and creative expression, making her a sought-after speaker and thought leader in English education.

An advocate for teacher-writers, Donovan founded initiatives like Ethical ELA, a website with free professional development. #VerseLove is an April event that provides teachers with supportive spaces to reflect and create through poetry. The #Verselove project won the 2024 Divergent Award. The Open

Write is a monthly writing group that developed protocols to guide students in reading with empathy, understanding trauma, and fostering healing. Her recent book projects, including 90 Ways of Community and Words That Mend, explore the therapeutic potential of poetry in educational settings and encourage teachers and students to write with authenticity and purpose.

Through her writing, mentorship, and public scholarship, Donovan continues to impact the field of secondary English education. Her work inspires educators to build classrooms that value each student's humanity, encourage resilience, and champion diverse voices. Her efforts to make literature a transformative experience position her as a leader in fostering inclusive, reflective learning environments that resonate deeply with both students and teachers.

PART I

1
Poetry in Our Digital World

Join us in stretching elements of poetry and technology—as we witness the ongoing crossover of the humanity of creativity applied through technology. Our framework will guide this movement away from scripted, mundane curricula and generic attempts at perpetuating sole consumption through digital settings. Are you willing to join us? Then read on.

The current state of writing instruction often neglects poetic form through limited or omitted standard requirements. We hope you, dear readers and fellow educators, enter this text as experts in content standards, with forward-thinking 21st-century mindsets, yet with a willingness to grow and disrupt your current practice. We will review elements of poetry and technology, along with how we devised our e-Poetry Framework in Part I. These ideas are presented for your consideration with our e-Poetry Framework in Part II.

Poetry is a form of expression, communication, and interpretation—agentive in the act of emotional response between reader and audience. It is meant to represent a moment, allow for witnessing, and unify lived experiences (Donovan & Boutelier, 2023; Forché, 1993; Weingarten, 2003). If we are to read the world, then we must transform and access not through trends but through modern means of communicative forms (Gregory, 2013). There are plenty of technology standards supported through multimedia and digital citizenry to transform this art.

Naji (2021) stated that the "art world itself is not clearly defined" and opens a field of practice for more practitioners, contributors, and audiences." This book accepts this undefined realm while acknowledging how often teachers want a measurable, static process.

This book meets at the intersection of ELA and technology. In an increasingly digital age, educators must adapt to meet the changing needs and interests of their students. We believe the craft of poetry helps humanize the art of expression, reflection, and analysis (even if poetry standards aren't explicit in many state standards). The chapters explore how poetry might present itself in a literacy-based unit with the benefit of a tech medium to then share with the world. We also consider the utilization of integrating tech (e.g., podcast as a literacy medium) and using poetry as the genre to master the said skills (e.g., podcasting).

Both poetry and technology lie in the margin, on the side, as add-ons in our K–12 curriculum. Without clear training, both are easily ignored and yet, ironically, easily added if one (i.e., the designer/educator) is interested or passionate about one or both. The authors are passionate about both. Through their own individual work and collaboration over the past five years, the authors bring forth their own experiences, expertise, and ongoing questions to share how digital poetry can be inspiring.

Why Poetry?

Poetry writing, reading, and revisioning elicit emotions through these experiences. Poetry tells history through time and crosses languages with purpose and worldly acknowledgment. Yet, often poetry is seen as elite, with a trope of poets, or as a type of writing not meant for the masses. However, poetry humanizes our words by connecting us through these common emotions and somatic experiences.

Throughout the ELA standards, state-to-state, you can search "poetry" with a quick CTRL-F. What you will find is "read and comprehend poetry" across most grade levels. What you will not find is "write" poetry. Instead, when considering what students should write in schools, there are standards related to writing narratives, arguments, and informational pieces. For example, students must "Write narratives to develop real or imagined experiences or events using effective technique, relevant descriptive details, and well-structured event sequences," or "Students will introduce a claim and organize reasons and evidence" for an argument or, for informational requirements, "Students will compose essays and reports to objectively introduce and develop topics, incorporating evidence (e.g., specific facts, examples, details, data)" (Oklahoma State Department of Education [OSDE], 2016). Maybe implied in these standards is that the form for these pieces of writing *could* be in poetic structure, but few textbooks seem to encourage teachers to make that connection.

Why is it that reading or analyzing poetry is worthwhile enough to name it as "important enough" to include in ELA instruction/classroom experiences but not the writing of poetry? Here are a few reasons to intentionally create opportunities for students to engage with composing poetry:

1. Writing poems welcomes creative self-expression (Jacobs, 2016; Raingruber, 2004). The many choices involved in crafting a poem offer students space to make decisions in lines, stanzas, word choice, topic, and length to say what they need to say and use white space for the things they may not be ready to say. Inviting students to write poetry honors their humanity by inviting their thoughts, emotions, and experiences into the classroom in abstract and imaginative ways that analytic essays and five-paragraph structures do not. To understand what form and structure can and cannot do, students need opportunities to write in a lot of different ways.
2. Writing poems refine language skills and consciousness. Writing poetry can enhance language skills such as vocabulary, metaphorical thinking, and symbolism.

It encourages students to play with words, experiment with language, and develop a deeper understanding of linguistic devices. Reading poetry is analytic in the naming of what they see poets doing, and when students are then invited to try those moves in their own poetry, they understand the linguistic features better (Baker & Mazza, 2004). Consider reading a recipe versus making the food. There is a greater understanding of the parts that make the whole.

3. Writing poetry positions students alongside the authors-poets they study. In other words, by positioning students as only ever writing about literature rather than creating literature, they may not see themselves as capable of or expected to contribute to the ideas and art in the world (Rowe, 2000). They can use music lyrics, social justice slam poems, or historical poems as mentor texts.

4. Writing poetry is not only about complex emotions and experiences; writing poetry can tell stories, inform readers about issues, and take a stand on issues to move readers' hearts, minds, and actions. The economy of words and craftful structure communicate in form and content experiences to witness and lessons worth considering (Connelly, 1999; Kreuter, 2009).

5. Writing poetry can serve our students' lives and ours (Baker & Mazza, 2004; Rowe, 2000). We don't see in the standards or textbooks much about how writing can benefit students as human beings, and that maybe writing need not be for school or a grade. There is value in writing poetry for the sake of writing poetry—the act of writing and creating is a way of being beyond the product or outcome. Writing poetry can be a cathartic process that helps students explore their identities, beliefs, and values. It fosters introspection and self-discovery, promoting personal growth and self-awareness.

All of these can be done with or without digital support for ongoing engagement and fostering of one's poet-self.

Why Technology?

Although this book is not about the history of technology or its takeover of educating humans in ways merely considered even years prior, we want to acknowledge some collective understandings before bridging into digital poetry. Technology definitions can date back to when our ancestors were using reeds, quills, and brushes to communicate (even through poetry) millennia ago. We could consider technology an accessibility innovation when braille was added to typewriters in the 19th century. However, for the sake of contemporary means, we will frame our reasoning around "why technology" from the lens of the need for developing global digitally moral citizens.

Digital citizenry has morphed over the last few decades, adjusting to novelties that stuck and those that were phased out (Ehrhardt et al., 2023). Connection to information and more importantly, other humans, is now more accessible, timely, and freer than it ever has been allowing for us to connect our students to experts around the world, artists in neighboring states, and students in different time zones. This potential is endless but doesn't come without action as the "citizen" part requires responsibility, empathy, and evaluation (see more on this in Chapter 2).

There may be technology scope and sequence plans in a district for K–12 meant to guide and scaffold digital skills, but these are often overlooked and not prioritized. Most often, educators just integrate tech because they like it, it is age-appropriate, or because it is new and shiny. Responsible use often starts with content before technology in one's pedagogical design. One might use the Substitution, Augmentation, Modification, Redefinition (SAMR) model, or one might align with the International Society for Technology in Education (ISTE) standards, or one might just go rogue and embed tech as they see fit. We are expert educators, after all.

The assumption is that students are coming into our classrooms with digital skills yet most often, they are solely consumers of digital content. We want them to be digital creators and critiquers. We are moving away from the phrase "digital

> **Box 1.1**
>
> SAMR for technology integration: Substitution, Augmentation, Modification, Redefinition (Puentedura, 2010)

native" (see Chapter 2) to a social life of multimodal audiences' temporality and permanency—our learners need to identify and analyze the differences to be successful and critical citizens. As you interact with this book, please consider these in relation to the *why* of technology:

- Why are we using technology? Does it redefine the learning environment and outcome? (See SAMR Box 1.1)
- How would you scaffold the ability to use a certain tech tool/app/software/hardware?
- When and why would you prioritize privacy in a digital setting?
- How would you maintain the necessary control over audiences (e.g., responses, shares)?
- How does this technology enhance literacy (i.e., poetry)?
- Why would you start with technology first (e.g., before content)?

Return to this as you consider the various ideas we share. Always think about the human element of education and how any e-Poetry lesson is designed with student-centered instruction.

Digital Poetry

In 2009, di Rosario explored e-Poetry and how it requires different practices of writing and reading from a humanities or English literary perspective. There are different genres of digital poetry (because of the medium, modalities, and situations), and those genres produce a new relationship with the "text"—one that engages an involved subject.

Digital poetry refers to poetic works that are created using digital technology, often displayed on electronic devices or computer screens. It can incorporate various multimedia elements, interactive features, and visual effects to enhance the poetic experience. There are various names for digital poetry: Machine poetry, cyber poetry, and techno poetry, which include algorithms, artificial intelligence (AI), rules, hypermedia, device variation, human-to-tech explorations, etc. For this book, we use the term *e-Poetry* to describe our framework and digital poetry to encompass the various interconnections of poetry and digital platforms (Edwards, 2015; Funkhouser, 2008; Gajjala & Oh, 2012). Publishing student-created digital poetry allows for: Cross-content connection, increased shareability, access to provide feedback, and feedback cycles. This book shares our digital poetry for tomorrow, as we (selves and texts) are always morphing based on trends and needs yet rooted in the creation of literacies today.

The term multimodal refers to the modes of meaning-making (i.e., audio, visual, linguistic, spatial, and gestural) integrated to create electronic multimedia texts (Cope & Kalantzis, 2000). Examples of digital writing include, but are not limited to, creating podcasts, creating and modifying wikis, writing and managing blogs, writing fan fiction, writing and digitally illustrating graphic novels, and creating mash-ups of existing audio, video, and texts for novel purposes. Digital writing has less to do with the medium with which the writer uses to compose and more to do with the ways in which writing is changing in response to new technologies. Grabill and Hicks (2005) use the term "digital writing" to refer to a "changed writing environment" (p. 304) that is characterized by connectivity that allows writers to access and share writing via the internet.

How This Book "Lives"

In ten years, will this book be a mere record of the evolution of digital literacies—will it still be relevant? All the research says not to teach grammar in isolation but in an authentic context (Anderson, 2023; Nosirova, 2023), so this book is about building meta-awareness of language through critical digital literacy.

This text is specifically designed for teachers at the secondary and higher education levels who are eager to explore the integration of e-Poetry and educational tech (ed tech) in their English, literature, creative writing, digital media courses, or in any literacy-centered unit. It also caters to teacher educators and curriculum designers seeking to incorporate these innovative methods into their teacher training programs. Standard alignment is through ELA, English Language Development (ELD), World-class Instructional Design and Assessment (WIDA), ISTE, Art, Digital Citizenship, and Multimedia Standards.

Here is how you can interact with this book:

1. Use it in class, use it for your own writing, and come back and interact with the content.
2. Go in order or out of order—this is for you.
3. Explore terms that are defined, referenced, and applied.
4. Design and play with the e-Poetry Framework (explored further in Chapter 3).
5. Acknowledge blending the non-neutrality and authenticity of digital poetry as an intentional pedagogy.

Digital poetry and many modern art forms are temporary (because of the limits and everchanging evolution of digital spaces and tools). Much of this is dependent on engagement. Your engagement and feedback throughout your interaction with this text will hopefully strengthen the evolution of digital poetry.

Overview of the Book

This book offers a comprehensive exploration of integrating digital literacies into classrooms, grounded in contemporary theories and practice. The following chapters guide educators through various approaches, tools, and frameworks to enhance student engagement, creativity, and critical thinking, all while addressing the ethical and equity considerations necessary for meaningful and responsible teaching in a digital age.

Depending on your comfort with poetry and technology, you can start at any chapter. However, understanding the e-Poetry Framework is essential to understanding the practical lessons, so we recommend reading Chapter 3 before diving into Part II's classroom ideas.

Part I
Chapter 2: *Digital Citizenry for Content Creators*
This chapter sets the stage by discussing the evolving concept of literacy, which now includes digital, visual, and AI literacies. Aligning with the National Council of Teachers of English (NCTE) 2018 beliefs, the chapter emphasizes the need to prioritize pedagogical goals and ethical considerations over the mere use of technology. By examining tools like e-Poetry and digital platforms, it illustrates how technology can foster creativity and critical thinking while ensuring that these innovations support equitable and inclusive teaching practices.

Chapter 3: *e-Poetry Framework: The Power of Choice in Digital Poetry Composition*
This chapter delves into the role of choice in the composition process, particularly within the context of e-Poetry. It presents a framework for authentic e-Poetry composition, emphasizing the importance of both student and teacher choices in shaping the learning experience. Through this framework, the chapter highlights how decisions about the purpose, mode, form, audience, interactivity, and permanence of digital content can foster student agency, engagement, and ethical considerations in digital composition.

Chapter 4: *From Draft to Digital: Understanding Writing Process Approaches to Poetry and Technology*
Focusing on the integration of poetry and technology through a writing process approach, this chapter offers practical steps for setting up a collaborative classroom environment. Grounded in established writing process theory and aligned with state standards, the chapter guides educators in fostering a creative space where both teachers and students engage in writing, revising, and publishing poetry. The use of mentor texts and the active participation of teachers in the writing process are emphasized as key elements of this approach.

Part II

Chapter 5: *Haiku in Motion: Celebrating School Community through GIF Poetry*

In this chapter, students explore the art of haiku writing through the creation of haiku GIFs that capture the essence of their school environment. This approach not only enhances literary and digital skills but also fosters a deeper connection to the school community. By turning hallways into sources of inspiration and sharing haiku GIFs on hallway TV broadcasts, students engage in a creative process that enriches school culture and promotes thoughtful decision-making in multimodal publishing.

Chapter 6: *Place-Based Poetry: Zip-Odes and YouTube Shorts*

This chapter explores place-based poetry with a focus on global and historical contexts, using zip-odes and YouTube Shorts to teach about Armenia's past and present. Students create zip-ode poems and digital shorts to reflect on their connections to places and understand the influence between places and people. The chapter demonstrates how these strategies can be applied to various topics, encouraging students to articulate their observations and emotions about impactful spaces.

Chapter 7: *AI + Nonet: Machine and Human Poetry Collaboration*

This chapter experiments with the intersection of AI and poetry by exploring the nonet form. It questions whether AI can truly emulate human creativity and emotional depth, providing examples and critiques that examine the role of AI in poetic creation. The chapter also offers insights and guided questions for educators on when and why AI might be used to support the poem-ing process.

Chapter 8: *Echoes of Persuasion: Two-Voiced Spoken Word Recordings*

Students begin by analyzing the rhetorical strategies of contemporary spoken word poetry, focusing on how artists use ethos, pathos, and logos to captivate audiences. They then apply these techniques to transform news stories into two-voiced, spoken word poems, highlighting overlooked perspectives and promoting missing voices in the news. The chapter emphasizes the importance of rhetorical impact and the role of technology in sharing students' work.

Chapter 9: *Concrete Piles of Positivity with Templates*
This chapter explores the visual and emotional impact of form through the creation of pile poems of good things, enhanced by digital templates like Canva. Educators are guided in designing templates that facilitate student engagement and creativity. The chapter also discusses the pedagogical benefits of using templates to scaffold learning and the importance of sharing and publishing digital student work.

Chapter 10: *Playing with Words: Enhancing Poetry Through Gamification*
The final chapter invites readers to explore the concept of gamifying digital poetry. It differentiates between gamification and game-based learning, illustrating how these concepts can be applied to the reading, creation, and analysis of poetry. Through various digital tools and methods, the chapter shows how to increase engagement in poem-ing online, offering a playful yet purposeful approach to digital poetry education.

Each chapter offers a different access point to the intersection of poetry and technology, providing a cohesive and practical guide for educators looking to integrate digital literacies into their ELA classrooms. By the end of the book, you will have a robust understanding of how to harness the power of technology to enhance literacy instruction while remaining grounded in ethical, inclusive, and humanizing teaching practices.

Reference List

Anderson, J. (2023). *Mechanically inclined: Building grammar, usage, and style into writer's workshop*. Routledge.

Baker, K. C., & Mazza, N. (2004). The healing power of writing: Applying the expressive/creative component of poetry therapy. *Journal of Poetry Therapy: The Interdisciplinary Journal of Practice, Theory, Research and Education, 17*(3), 141–154.

Connelly, J. (1999). Being in the present moment: Developing the capacity for mindfulness in medicine. *Academic Medicine, 74,* 420–424.

Cope, B., & Kalantzis, M. (Eds.). (2000). *Multiliteracies: Literacy learning and the design of social futures.* Routledge.

di Rosario, G. (2009). Digital poetry: A naissance of a new genre? *Carnets, 20,* 183–205. https://doi.org/10.4000/carnets.3762

Donovan, S., & Boutelier, S. (2023). Human-centered Poem-ing: The care of teacher-writers online. *Writing & Pedagogy, 15*(1–2), 73–90. https://doi.org/10.1558/wap.24337

Edwards, J. D. (2015). *Technologies of the Gothic in literature and culture-technogothics.* Routledge.

Ehrhardt, S. G., Babwahab, S., Skopnik, H., & Schmiedgen, M. (2023). Mortality prediction in patients with ARDS: A pragmatic tool for bedside risk stratification. *Frontiers in Medicine, 10,* Article 10480606. https://doi.org/10.3389/fmed.2023.10480606

Forché, C. (1993). *Against forgetting: Twentieth-century poetry of witness.* W. W. Norton.

Funkhouser, C. (2008). Digital poetry: A look at generative, visual, and interconnected possibilities in its first four decades. In R. Siemens & S. Schreibman (Eds.), *A companion to digital literary studies,* chapter 17. Blackwell. https://companions.digitalhumanities.org/DLS/

Gajjala, R., & Oh, Y. J. (2012). *Cyberfeminism 2.0.* Peter Lang.

Grabill, J. T., & Hicks, T. (2005). Multiliteracies meet methods: The case for digital writing in English education. *English Education, 37*(4), 301–311.

Gregory, H. (2013). Youth take the lead: Digital poetry and the next generation. *English in Education, 47,* 118–133. https://doi.org/10.1111/eie.12011

Jacobs, B. (2016). The creative journal: The art of finding yourself. *Journal of Poetry Therapy: The Interdisciplinary Journal of Practice, Theory, Research and Education, 29*(3), 183–184.

Kreuter, E. A. (2009). Catalyzing the inner spirit of the type-A professional through poetic expression. *Journal of Poetry Therapy: The Interdisciplinary Journal of Practice, Theory, Research and Education, 22*(3), 165–171.

Naji, J. (2021). *Digital poetry.* Palgrave Macmillan. https://doi.org/10.1007/978-3-030-65962-2

Nosirova, D. (2023). Learning grammar through context: Enhancing language proficiency. *Modern Science and Research*, *2*(7), 349–351.

Oklahoma State Department of Education. (2016). *Oklahoma academic standards for English language arts*. OSDE. (Final Version). https://sde.ok.gov/sites/default/files/documents/files/OAS-ELA-Final%20Version_0.pdf

Puentedura, R. (2010). SAMR and TPCK: Intro to advanced practice. http://hippasus.com/resources/sweden2010/SAMR_TPCK_IntroToAdvancedPractice.pdf

Raingruber, B. (2004). Using poetry to discover and share significant meanings in child and adolescent mental health nursing. *Journal of Child and Adolescent Psychiatric Nursing*, *17*(1), 13–20.

Rowe, R. C. (2000). Poetry and verse: An ideal medium for scientific communication. *Drug Discovery Today*, *5*(10), 436–437.

Weingarten, K. (2003). *Common shock: Witnessing violence every day: How we are harmed, how we can heal*. Penguin Group.

2

Digital Citizenry for Content Creators

> *a symphony of words in the digital age*
>   *across the tomes, texts, and tools*
> *computer-created poetry–human or ai*
>   *where lies the essence of poetry*
>   *concrete poetry's multimodal realm*
> *cyber-poetry*
>   *unleashing writers as their own publishers*
>   *agency granted, but without peer review or ethical gates*
> *a dance with genre*
>   *defying audience, form, medium, and situation*
>   *print on paper transfers to the web*
> *consumption*
>   *dance between verbal text and audio-visual images*
>   *a new avant-garde genre unfolds*
> *digital collaboration*
>   *rewrites its existence.*
>   *a relationality beyond democratic pedagogy*
>   *readers not just participating but involved*
> *echoes of the present*
>   *mechanical creation devalues the individual*
>   *generative work defined in tech terms*
> *transparency eludes*
>   *is this the essence of e-poetry?*
>   *the internet, a productive medium,*
> *a focus beyond literary creation,*
>   *students as authors of text generators*
>   *a new relation in the triad of sender-message-receiver*
> *digital evolutions*
>   *multimodality, cultural diversity, social justice*
>   *consuming, producing, new relationship*

> *beyond the confines of text*
> *   hyperlinks, audio, video, choose your adventure*
> *   temporal realms of digital genres*
> *genre as language*
> *   unneutral technologies*
> *   a symphonic techno-tapestry unfolds*

We put in a first, unedited draft of this chapter into ChatGPT4o and requested it to produce a free verse poem. We received a poem that we then edited for the opening of this chapter. All the language and concepts are ours—put into AI but reorganized to create a new perspective.

Current generations (some are using Zillennial to encompass both Gen Z and Millennials) have lived life on the grid. Shorts, GIFs, and online media creations are their new language. Our permanence and history-making are rebuilt through our digital selves. This feeds into information that is a self/human post or a third-party/machine distribution. This ongoing process includes the distribution, collection, and potential manipulation of personal data on the journey as we become digitally literate. All posts and digital interactions pose risks that can be ethically, monetarily, socially, professionally, or emotionally damaging. Moral digital citizenship must be part of any practice that includes tech to enhance engagement and creativity, social responsibility, and empathy in any digital setting. Being a global digital citizen also includes considerations around literacies, accessibility, equity, and inclusivity.

Our learning and experiences are enhanced with technology as our classrooms and education must involve digital literacies to stay connected. This book aligns with the National Council for Teachers of English (NCTE)'s (2018) Beliefs for Integrating Technology into the ELA classroom to help illuminate the technology-driven decisions we, as educators, make. These are decisions related to design, engagements in public media spaces, and understanding how literacies promote or detract from ethical, human-centered digital citizenry. Educators must be experts in the various literacies as well to support both ourselves and our students' development. We provide context and connection to each of the beliefs.

Literacy Means Literacies

Crovitz et al. (2022) centered around "real-world digital scenarios" to engage and inspire students. The rhetorical and critical helps teachers see the ethical implications of consuming and producing digital texts, and this book attends to the language—to "understand and change the world" and with consideration of "linguistic and cultural appropriation in digital contexts."

There are Literacy Standards: reading, writing, listening and speaking. There is the craft of writing, the workshopping, and the personal literacies that flow throughout these cycles. There are poetry analyses and verse novels that support literacies without stated standards. We can evaluate critical literacy and creative literacy. Digital literacies, visual literacy, math literacy, and now AI Literacy (Nash et al., 2023) remind us of the multitude and endless literacies around us.

That moves us to multimodal standards, where the digital, science, art-making, and inquiry cycles continue to flood the processes. This might look like memes, podcasts, infographics, artistic forms of creation, making literature, interpreting, and remixing. Some states now have multimodal standards, like Oklahoma's Multimodal Literacies (OSDE, n.d.) Standard 7, which includes reading and writing multimodal content across grade levels (see Table 2.1)

It can take some time for the research to be formalized into standards, but often, the standards spark a need for professional development and a surge of new scholarship to support teachers in reimagining their practices. The International Society for Technology in Education (ISTE, 2024a) Standards for educators and students focus on designer skills and becoming a collaborator in one's learning process as 21st-century skills and not a single focus on "tech" literacy.

Consider Literacies before Technologies

All experienced and novice educators should be versed in the process of pedagogy/content before technology. Yet, we can

TABLE 2.1 Multimodal Literacies Standard Across Grade Levels

Grade	Standard#	Standard Language
6th Grade	7.6.R.1	Students will compare and contrast the effectiveness of a variety of written, oral, visual, digital, nonverbal, and interactive texts to generate and answer questions and create new understandings.
7th Grade	7.7.R.1	Students will compare and contrast the effectiveness of techniques used in a variety of written, oral, visual, digital, nonverbal, and interactive texts to generate and answer questions and create new understandings.
8th Grade	7.8.R.1	Students will analyze and evaluate the effectiveness of techniques used in written, oral, visual, digital, nonverbal, and interactive texts with a focus on persuasion and argument to generate and answer questions and create new understandings.
9th Grade	7.9.R.1	Students will determine the intended purposes of the tools and techniques used for rhetorical effects in written, oral, visual, digital, nonverbal, and interactive texts to generate and answer questions and create new understandings.
10th Grade	7.10.R.1	Students will analyze the tools and techniques used to achieve the intended rhetorical purposes in written, oral, visual, digital, nonverbal, and interactive texts to generate and answer questions and create new understandings.
11th Grade	7.11.R.1	Students will analyze and evaluate the various ways visual image-makers construct arguments in written, oral, visual, digital, nonverbal, and interactive texts to generate and answer questions and create new understandings.
12th Grade	7.12.R.1	Students will analyze and evaluate written, oral, visual, digital, nonverbal, and interactive texts in order to draw conclusions and defend arguments.

welcome how literacies (e.g., poetry) can help us understand technology or how we can create a deeper connection with our audience through digital means (Barnes & Marlatt, 2024; Barnwell, 2023; Hicks, 2021; Hicks & Runstrom, 2023; Lisenbee et al., 2020). Digital poetry can take classroom learning into extended communities and share it with authentic audiences. Educators have their own set of ISTE standards (different from

> **Box 2.1**
>
> UDL (Universal Design for Learning) guides learning facilitators to design to support all learners and increase accessibility. All educators should consider UDL's principles of Representation, Action and Expression, and Engagement when designing to support the agency of all learners. WCAG (Web Content Accessibility Guidelines) guides designers to use the correct accessibility tools for sharing and facilitating in digital spaces (CAST, 2024; W3C, 2023).

student standards) to prioritize literacies (i.e., learner, designer, facilitator, analyst, collaborator, leader, and citizenship) before technology.

Even if digital writing is solely text-based, text in a digital environment has the potential to be far more dynamic than just black letters on a white page. Words in a digital space can change size and color and can be animated with movements to emphasize their meaning or sustain the reader's attention (e.g., access, UDL 3.0, WCAG 2.2, see Box 2.1). These compositions can range from basic word processing on one end of the continuum to multimodal text production using Web 2.0 interfaces (i.e., advancement to user-generated content) on the other end.

Technologies Provide New Ways to Consume and Produce Texts

Kajder (2010) called for a shift, we are always calling for growth, for teachers to be alongside students doing inquiry afforded by and through technologies. Being a 21st-century English teacher involves imagining reading and writing multimodal texts and participatory media. Students now carry their devices with them as an extension of their being. These devices can hold books in digital form, allow for immediate feedback, and encourage quick edits. These devices have become an extension of our being, how we witness and how we humanize tech access (Donovan & Boutelier, 2023; Forché, 1993; Weingarten, 2003). Digital poetry can be considered a reflexive practice, building upon previous literacies for consumption and production as experimentation and permanence (Naji, 2019).

Technologies and their Associated Literacies are not Neutral

Why digital poetry? Angello (2015) believes:

> Because of the constantly changing nature of digital media, has a unique opportunity to act as a site of micropolitical resistance. It can disrupt the relationships that cultural producers have to the systems within which they work because of its uniquely short life, and a growing number of poets working in digital media are embracing this fact.
> (p. 26)

Youth are focused on identity through digital exploration and use their devices for change (or staticity) through the potential of online civic identities through the "app" language (Abramova & Antonova, 2023; Gardner & Davis, 2013).

There is something about "online" and the new ways to consume and produce texts. The ways are not neutral but fundamentally bound to equity considering: Who has access (Wi-Fi equity) to what version (updates, pay vs. free subscription), on what device (varies), how much energy does it demand or carry (electricity or solar), and for whom is the content (age appropriateness, influencing to do and think what and why).

We can call digital texts temporary art or temporary texts in that while they may not be designed to be accessible for only a short period of time, the genre, platform, and access could be dissolved, remixed, or replaced at any time. Whereas traditional writing is characterized by being "static, linear, individually created, and print-based," writing with digital tools creates the potential for writing to be "fluid, dynamic, nonlinear, and often collaboratively constructed" (Curwood et al., 2013, p. 678).

Multi-Digital Art Forms

How do we use human experience and technology to create poetry in digital spaces for meaningful creation, dissemination, and experience for both reader and audience? di Rosario (2009) explores e-Poetry, asking if it is, in fact, a new genre and its own digital art form. Hayles (2008) names several forms/genres/modes of digital art: 1) Flash poetry; 2) visual e-Poetry; 3) digital poetry with passive interaction; 4) digital poetry with active interaction; 5) generative e-Poetry; 6) collaborative e-Poetry; 7) and ASCII (American Standard Code for Information Interchange) poems focused on code. Dalton and Proctor (2014) identify four types of digital text:

1. Linear in digital format (predictable, narrative-like structures)
2. Nonlinear texts with hyperlinks (supplemental information)
3. Texts with integrated media (accessible, multimodal experience)
4. Texts with response options (interactive, fluid literacy)

Understanding how these look and work is an essential part of digital literacy and designing digital poetry. These "literacies" are often described as multimodal (the process and intentional design of digital poetry) and multimedia (the digital art outcome). They both support the mode of meaning, meaning-making systems, or how people create meaning. The Cazden et al. (1996, p. 80) categorizes these multi-art forms as:

♦ Visual meaning with still and moving images with color, page layout, shot framing, angels, camera movement, and subject movement; linguistic meaning is spoken and

written language in word choice, discourse(s) norms, syntax, mechanics
- Aural meaning is sound and silence with volume, pitch, rhythm (music, sound effects)
- Spatial meaning concerns environmental and architectural spaces and the use of proximity, direction, and position of objects in space
- Gestural meaning invokes movement of the body, facial expression, demeanor, body language, speed, stillness, position, nonverbal

These overlay with Dalton and Proctor's (2014) digital text descriptors. Therefore, considering multimodality as a combination or integration of various communication modes as we learn, facilitate, and design leads to the creation of a multimedia output (e.g., the interface of visual images alongside the written word; a television show has unique gestural, aural, and visual meanings that the script for the show does not).

Digital Citizenry

We are committed to the creative act of crafting poetry in a safe, sustainable manner through digital poetry. We have access to non-static digital tools to design or create with to humanize the digital learning environment. Publishing this book is important as we are adding to the footprint now—adding this "living" element demonstrates and collects evidence of the changes along the way (for critique or celebration). Give yourself permission to use technology, be creative, have fun, make mistakes, and show students that things don't always work the first time with tech.

It is difficult to envision any space without the use of modern technology. I have a lesson assignment in one of my courses requiring pre-service and in-service educators to write a "non-tech" lesson. I limit the specifications aside from their previous knowledge of the instructional design (in this case, backward planning). Almost all educators submit a first draft of this lesson with a tech component (submitting the lesson in a digital doc doesn't count). The common flaw is that the content is presented to learners via a tech tool (e.g., computer to classroom screen), but learners aren't holding a device. This process allows us to realize how often we rely on technology to support our curriculum and how difficult it is to avoid it. Using a screen, for example, with content presented in multiple ways is a useful UDL Principle of Representation and aligns with ISTE Educator Standard 5: Designer (ISTE, 2024a). The point is that we are always using technology and it is more difficult to move completely away from it.

Another reminder of the power of online access is how using Flip (this tool is now longer available as a free video platform) or other video tools (both synchronous and asynchronous) allows us to create digital communities and connect students across the world. This experience is empowering and embodies the element of humanizing the machine. This reinforces the power, need, and avoidance of technology in our lives.

This section will explore a variety of perspectives related to digital ethics and how they overlap with elements of our framework. Currently, national laws address stricter restrictions for those learners who are 12 and under (e.g., Children's Online Privacy Protection Act [COPPA]). Access and information collection increases at the age of 13 for now (see section for pending legislation, APRA, n.d.). Since this book is focused on secondary ELA classes, we will allow your expertise in knowing the age of your students, understanding your district (e.g., media compliance and guardian signage), state, and national laws to apply to your practice. All examples and discussions going forth apply to learners aged 13 and over—please practice and design responsibly.

ISTE (n.d.) provides the Teacher Ready Evaluation Tool for us to evaluate tools for agency, accessibility, assessment, etc., and puts us in the expert seat—thank you. You can self-evaluate a tool (separated into three product types: Assessment, curriculum, and platform). This puts ownership on us and a responsibility as expert pedagogues to know what tools we use to support our design. This is imperative for the role of modeling digital ethics.

Our digital world is rarely separated from our daily lives—at all ages. Digital addiction is plaguing us in ways we could not have anticipated. Many schools are banning personal cell/smartphones in K–12 settings (e.g., California legislature); however, even with these modern extensions of our being, we are distracted (Almourad et al., 2020; Ding & Li, 2023; Kross et al., 2021; Maza et al., 2023). Our distraction is plagued by: What am I missing? Did someone need me? Was there a notification? What is the weather today even though I am standing outside? Psychologists note that the only way to combat digital addiction is to use tech tools to do so (Addiction Center, n.d.; Karakose et al., 2023). This would include using specified apps for turning off notifications, apps to limit timing, and programs to move our eyes from the screen. Adults are having this issue, and our brains are being re-wired with technology utilized in every aspect of our lives—we can barely flourish without access to technology in today's world—what will tomorrow bring (Alcott et al., 2021)?

The importance of moderating, critiquing, and creating is built from our obsession with technology and is a needed skill that is now required. We cannot avoid technology, but we must understand how to balance and remain human social beings, as we must prepare our students for responsible digital citizenry. Our students will graduate high school and college and need a skill set that cannot be easily fulfilled by AI (think entry-level jobs). We feel this is important to point out in this book because we are promoting the utilization of technology and the ongoing consideration of how we do and should use it in our classrooms. We will highlight elements of digital citizenship, privacy, and safety for considerations along the way of using the e-Poetry Framework, ultimately making sense of using tech from a human/ethical perspective.

We ask, are you tech-able (able to align tech efficiency and are teachable in needed updates)? Are our students tech-able? This is a broad skill set for using technology to thrive in the future world. Does your district, classroom, and teacher-self acknowledge the relevance of digital media in the modern ELA curriculum? We assume yes if you've made it this far in our book. Understanding the various types of digital media and how they

> **Box 2.2**
>
> Digital Citizenship includes necessary 21st century skills for healthy digital balance, anti-bullying, responsible communication, media literacy, privacy, and long-term implications (Common Sense Education, n.d.)

utilize our data is important as an educator for your own online safety and particularly for your students' permanent digital footprint (ISTE, 2024b, see Box 2.2). The ISTE DigCit Commit competencies are an important parallel to our centering humans in this process—any process where technology is involved. If one proclaims they are a breathing human in the digital world, then they should commit to being (ISTE, 2024b):

- Inclusive: Engage with others online with respect and empathy
- Informed: Evaluate the accuracy, perspective, and validity of online information
- Engaged: Use technology for civic engagement and to be a force for good
- Balanced: Prioritize my time and activities online and offline
- Alert: Know how to be safe online and create safe spaces for others

Digital Privacy and Safety

These two, digital privacy and safety, are difficult to separate. How do we keep our online information private, and how safe is it to input some of our personal information on digital platforms? Personal data includes, but is not limited to, full names, phone numbers, addresses, government-issued identification numbers, and images. All of this seems to be curated from an early age (e.g., if parents post and name pictures of their children on socials) to begin building one's digital footprint, digital image, or digital evidence. This piece alone—making sure students understand the permanence of posting online—is an initial element expanded earlier. As some call it, a digital shadow might haunt a person their entire life. We've seen plenty of instances in the media where bullying, blackmailing, typecasting, etc., are built from this digital story permanently ready to share and be searched. These are common privacy risks for students and teachers. Therefore, we must address protection for everyone through learning, mentoring, and modeling.

Legal and Ethical Considerations
There are federal laws protecting student privacy that are mandated in public settings, plus there are state and district-based elements that must also be considered. COPPA student privacy laws date back to 1998, with the latest updates in 2013. There are legislative proposals and updates in 2024 (Federal Trade Commission [FTC], 2023). Included in this bill and other proposals, online companies would be banned from collecting personal information for 13–17-year-olds (Jalonick, 2024). COPPA is aimed at the privacy of students under age 13 for software, school district mandates for parental consent, etc. (see COPPA checklist at Iubenda, n.d.). This also includes the expectation that the age of 13 is the minimum (not necessarily required age) for social media accounts (e.g., Meta, TikTok, see National Education Association, n.d., https://www.nea.org/social-media). This will be the first update in decades and will include options to delete minor's personal information and reroute advertising for those aged 17 and under (Jalonick, 2024).

We must also consider the Family Educational Rights and Privacy Act (FERPA), which is meant to allow parents of children 17 and under or students 18 and over to have a say in what information is shared with others (particularly third-party programming, think about those websites that ask your age) (U.S. Department of Education, n.d.). The newest government-issued "Kids Online Health and Safety Report" (National Telecommunications and Information Administrations, 2024) states:

> …'safety' encompasses protection from harms in both the online and physical worlds that youth may experience

because of online engagement and interactions. Youth face a multitude of safety issues and associated harms online: they range from cyberbullying and online harassment, to encouraging self-harm, to grooming and child sexual exploitation. Much of the research on safety has focused on quantifying these harms—such as when youth of different ages encounter violence online or sextortion, and there is less material on the efficacy of different measures to keep kids safe. Importantly, these risks to safety affect both youth's physical and mental health.

(p. 12)

We now have most websites in the US asking us to "accept" their cookie-stealing/sharing settings (Europe was way ahead of the US on these requirements). We (i.e., USA) finally have The American Privacy Act of 2024 moving through the legislature as well. Ethical use of student data is imperative to consider when designing and implementing any curriculum. We advise you to learn and follow the district, state, and government policies required at your school.

Equity

The definition of digital equity once centered on 1:1 access (e.g., Chromebooks for everyone!). Then, during COVID-19 we considered digital access to include Wi-Fi, bandwidth, and the mobility of devices. We must still consider the latter if we require not only digital creation outside of the school but also how each school sets up their IT permissions. This cannot be avoided and must be part of any digital poetry process.

We cannot micromanage the devices or apps that our teenage students use (screenshots or picture taking of work should follow fair use protocols), but we can return to the earlier elements in this chapter to consider how we model, discuss, and guide technology along with the learning that is taking place in our classrooms. We can advocate for equitable access and define those terms for our learners. We must learn about who is "watching" or "commenting" on different platforms by learning how to view analytics (with specific tools) and having objectives that live with modern digital citizenship ethics at the forefront to continue to consider digital equity.

Privacy Risks in Digital Poetry Projects

The e-Poetry Framework intentionally includes the consideration of permanence in the digital tool process (see more in Chapter 3). This gets us to consider (but not be perfect in) how we inadvertently share personal information and use third-party platforms. One example of this is the Canva privacy policy (n.d.). In this policy, a child is considered a person under the age of 13 years old (or the minimum legal age in the child's country to be able to provide lawful consent to the processing of their personal data where the age is higher than 13 years old). Some websites allow usage without an email login (which might be its own privacy concern but not elaborated here). Here are common best practices for protecting student privacy:

- Educating/modeling students about online privacy
- Setting classroom guidelines for digital projects previewing/testing/sharing of platforms
- Criteria for selecting digital tools
- Choose safe and secure platforms; recommended platforms with strong privacy policies
- Learn how to find the privacy features of each tool
- Know the legal policies and expectations
- Know the media policy that your learners' adults signed

Throughout the book, you will see a multitude of examples of technology used but always return to creating Privacy-Aware Digital Poetry Assignments.

Ethical Publication Practices

We will not expand much on these topics (we know you either know these or can search for your own guidance) but we acknowledge the importance of being ethical digital citizens by giving credit where it is due and protecting our creations. We encourage you to become familiar with appropriate copyright, fair use, Creative Commons, citing requirements (e.g., APA, MLA) for your own work, to mentor and model for your students (ISTE, 2024a), and when using others words (e.g., https://owl.purdue.edu/owl/general_writing/punctuation/quotation_marks/quotation_marks_with_fiction.html; see OWL Purdue, 2024).

Artificial Intelligence

The topic of AI continues to bring forth the dichotomy between machine and emotion. Can a machine provide output with emotion? Is that needed for poetry or any narrative writing? Educators and students might have a variety of reasons to knowingly or unconsciously use AI. AI expertise is still emerging, meaning educators and learners are still navigating how AI might play out in our learning. AI tools are improving and expanding every day (see Chapter 7), and it is difficult to separate ed tech and AI these days. Most educational technology tools have an AI component (e.g., Canva, Google). We cannot avoid it; we must critique and collaborate. Stefani explored AI through co-learning and addressing how and when to use AI appropriately. We are no longer teaching "digital natives," first named by Prensky (2001), with language that is outdated and offensive. Now, we are teaching the digital consumer, where educators are the digital appliers, and technology (AI) plays a role as a digital generator (Vredevoogd & Boutelier, 2024). AI should not be misused, but it cannot be avoided. We must identify the difference between AI theory and AI tools—what piece are we resisting in relation to this (see Table 2.2)?

TABLE 2.2 AI Theory vs. Tools. What Is Posing the Challenges, Resistance, or Conveniences?

AI Theory: Examples	AI Tools: Examples
Turing Test: Can the machine act and respond on its own	GAI: Generative AI (large language models or LLMs)
AGI: Artificial General Intelligence	Predictive AI: Assistive tools (e.g., predictive text)
AI Hallucinations (fake, incorrect outputs from AI)	Evaluative AI: Assessment tools (e.g., Grammarly)

Generative AI (e.g., Llama, Gemini, ChatGPT) also falls under the 13-year-old safety and privacy requirements. Many AI policies are currently centered on punitive measures and not as much on its ethical utility as a tech tool. This is important to note in this chapter since it is changing daily and gives reason why we must consider the immediacy of this topic.

Digital Reflection

In concluding this chapter, we have delved into the complex interplay between technology and ethics, with a specific focus on media literacy as it relates to the subsequent chapters on e-Poetry. This exploration has illuminated how multimodality and multimedia have fundamentally altered traditional practices and relationships within literature and education. The shift from print to digital media has not only expanded the boundaries of genres and modes of creative expression but has also challenged established norms of authorship, participation, and literacy. And with that comes or has come issues of ethics and safety that are especially important when working with students under 13 for legal reasons and 13 and over to inform their choices. The integration of digital environments necessitates a rethinking of our engagement with texts, as these new modalities blur the distinctions between consuming and producing content. Indeed, the subsequent chapters focus on analyzing content to inform and shape the content students create. This technological evolution offers unprecedented opportunities for creative and communicative advancements, yet it simultaneously introduces significant concerns regarding privacy, equity, and ethical use.

The chapter highlights the crucial need for developing digital citizenship and literacy skills in students, equipping them for a future where technological proficiency is indispensable. Educators are called to model and impart responsible technology use, striking a balance between leveraging digital tools and addressing privacy and ethical issues. This includes an understanding of legal frameworks such as COPPA and FERPA and staying abreast of evolving policies and best practices. Rather than viewing technology as an adjunct to traditional methods, it should be recognized as a transformative force that redefines educational experiences and prepares students for emerging challenges. As we navigate these digital innovations, our ultimate aim is to foster a learning environment that is not only advanced in its use of technology but also grounded in ethical considerations and inclusivity, ensuring that all students benefit from a thoughtful and responsible integration of digital tools.

Reference List

Abramova, S. B., & Antonova, N. L. (2023). Regional youth in search of civic identity: Digital participation and the observer model. *Sociology of Education in the Regions, 31*(2), 393–410. https://doi.org/10.15507/2413-1407.123.031.202302.393-410

Addiction Center. (n.d.). *Treatment for technology addiction.* https://www.addictioncenter.com/behavioral-addictions/treatment-technology-addiction/

Alcott, H., Gentzkow, M., & Song, L. (June 2021). Digital addiction (working paper No. 21-037). *SIEPR Stanford Institute for Economic Policy Research.* sieper.stanford.edu

Almourad, M. B., McAlaney, J., Skinner, T., Pleva, M., & Ali, R. (2020). Defining digital addiction: Key features from the literature. *Psihologija, 53*(3), 237–253.

American Privacy Rights Act of 2024, APRA. (n.d.). *APRA section by section* [PDF]. https://d1dth6e84htgma.cloudfront.net/APRA_Section_by_Section_026cc46a2c.pdf

Angello, A. (2015). To archive or not to archive: The resistant potential of digital poetry. *Text Matters, 5.* https://doi.org/10.1515/texmat-2015-0002

Barnes, M. E., & Marlatt, R. (Eds.). (2024). *Teaching for equity, justice, and antiracism with digital literacy practices: Knowledge, tools, and strategies for the ELA classroom.* Taylor and Francis.

Barnwell, P. (2023). Embracing technologies with purpose. *Council Chronicle, 33*(1), 28–33.

Canva. (n.d.). *Privacy policy.* https://www.canva.com/policies/privacy-policy/

CAST. (2024). Universal design for learning guidelines version 3.0. Retrieved from https://udlguidelines.cast.org

Cazden, C., Cope, B., Fairclough, N., Gee, J., et al.; New London Group. (1996). A pedagogy of multiliteracies: Designing social futures. *Harvard Educational Review*, *66*(1), 60–92.

Common Sense Education. (n.d.). *Digital citizenship*. https://www.commonsense.org/education/digital-citizenship

Crovitz, D., Devereaux, M. D., & Moran, C. M. (2022). *Next level grammar for a digital age: Teaching with social media and online tools for rhetorical understanding and critical creation*. Routledge.

Curwood, J. S., Magnifico, A. M., & Lammers, J. C. (2013). Writing in the wild: Writers' motivation in fan-based affinity spaces. *Journal of Adolescent & Adult Literacy*, *56*(8), 677–685. https://doi.org/10.1002/JAAL.192

Dalton, B., & Proctor, C. P. (2014). The changing landscape of text and comprehension in the age of new literacies. In J. Coiro, M. Knobel, C. Lankshear, & D. J. Leu (Eds.), *Handbook of Research on New Literacies* (pp. 297–324). Routledge

di Rosario, G. (2009). Digital poetry: A naissance of a new genre? *Carnets*, *20*, 183–205. https://doi.org/10.4000/carnets.3762

Ding, K., & Li, H. (2023). Digital addiction intervention for children and adolescents: A scoping review. *International Journal of Environmental Research and Public Health*, *20*(6), 4777. https://doi.org/10.3390/ijerph20064777

Donovan, S. & Boutelier, S. (2023). Human-centered Poem-ing: The care of teacher-writers online. *Writing & Pedagogy*, *15*(1–2), 73–90. https://doi.org/10.1558/wap.24337

Forché, C. (1993). *Against forgetting: Twentieth-century poetry of witness*. W. W. Norton.

Federal Trade Commission. (2023). RIN3084-AB20 children's online privacy protection rule. FTC. Retrieved from https://www.govinfo.gov/content/pkg/FR-2024-01-11/pdf/2023-28569.pdf

Gardner, H., & Davis, K. (2013). *The app generation: How today's youth navigate identity, intimacy, and imagination in a digital world* (1st ed.). Yale University Press. https://doi.org/10.12987/9780300199185

Hayles, K. (2008). *Electronic literature: New horizons for the literary*. University of Notre Dame Press.

International Society for Technology in Education. (2024a). *ISTE educator standards*. ISTE. https://iste.org/standards/educators

International Society for Technology in Education. (n.d.). *ISTE standards: Test version*. ISTE. https://tr-test.iste.org/

International Society for Technology in Education. (2024b). *Digital citizenship*. ISTE. https://iste.org/digital-citizenship

Iubenda. (n.d.). *COPPA compliance checklist*. https://www.iubenda.com/en/help/113898-coppa-compliance-checklist

Hicks, T. (2021). *Mindful teaching with technology: Digital diligence in the English language arts, grades 6–12*. Guilford Publications.

Hicks, T., & Runstrom, J. (2023). *Literacies before technologies*. ncte. org.

Jalonick, M. C. (2024, May 17). *Senate passes bill to boost child safety online*. AP News. https://apnews.com/article/senate-child-safety-online-schumer-59c7f67645afaaa7354f914f394ba652

Kajder, S. (2010). *Adolescents and digital literacies: Learning alongside our students (Principles in Practice)*. NCTE.

Karakose, T., Yıldırım, B., Tülübaş, T., & Kardas, A. (2023). A comprehensive review on emerging trends in the dynamic evolution of digital addiction and depression. *Frontiers in Psychology, 14*, 1126815.

Kross, E., Verduyn, P., Sheppes, G., Costello, C. K., Jonides, J., & Ybarra, O. (2021). Social media and well-being: Pitfalls, progress, and next steps. *Trends in Cognitive Sciences, 25*(1), 55–66. https://doi.org/10.1016/j.tics.2020.10.005

Lisenbee, P., Pilgrim, J., & Vasinda, S. (2020). *Integrating technology in literacy instruction: Models and frameworks for all learners*. Routledge.

Maza, M. T., Fox, K. A., Kwon, S. J., Flannery, J. E., Lindquist, K. A., Prinstein, M. J., & Telzer, E. H. (2023). Association of habitual checking behaviors on social media with longitudinal functional brain development. *JAMA Pediatrics, 177*(2), 160–167. https://doi.org/10.1001/jamapediatrics.2022.4924

Naji, J. (2019). The art of machine use subversion in digital poetry. *Hyperrhiz: New Media Cultures, 21*. https://doi.org/10.20415/hyp/021.e04

Nash, B. L., Hicks, T., Garcia, M., Fassbender, W., Alvermann, D., Boutelier, S., McBride, C., McGrail, E., Moran, C., O'Byrne, I., Piotrowski, A., Rice, M., & Young, C. (2023). Artificial intelligence in English education: Challenges and opportunities for teachers and teacher educators. *English Education, 55*(3), 201–206.

National Education Association. (n.d.). *Social media*. NEA. https://www.nea.org/social-media

National Council of Teachers of English. (2018, October 25). *Beliefs for integrating technology into the English language arts classroom.* NCTE. https://ncte.org/statement/beliefs-technology-preparation-english-teachers/

National Telecommunications and Information Administration. (2024). *Kids online health and safety: Report* [PDF]. U.S. Department of Commerce. https://www.ntia.gov/sites/default/files/reports/kids-online-health-safety/2024-kohs-report.pdf

Oklahoma State Department of Education. (n.d.). *Oklahoma academic standards for English language arts: Standard 7 (3rd draft).* OSDE. https://sde.ok.gov/sites/ok.gov.sde/files/documents/files/3rddraftstandard7.pdf

OWL Purdue. (2024). Quoting poetry. Retrieved August 5, 2024 from https://owl.purdue.edu/owl/general_writing/punctuation/quotation_marks/quotation_marks_with_fiction.html

Prensky, M. (2001). Digital natives, digital immigrants. *On the Horizon, 9*(5), 1–6. Retrieved January 28, 2009 from http://www.scribd.com/doc/9799/Prensky-Digital-Natives-Digital-Immigrants-Part1. Archived at http://www.webcitation.org/5eBDYI5Uw

U.S. Department of Education. (n.d.). *Family Educational Rights and Privacy Act (FERPA).* https://www2.ed.gov/policy/gen/guid/fpco/ferpa/index.html

Vredevoogd, I., & Boutelier, S. (2024). Co-learning with AI in the ELA classroom. In C. Moran (Ed.), *Revolutionizing English Education: AI in the Classroom* (pp. 157–175). Rowman and Littlefield.

Weingarten, K. (2003). *Common shock: Witnessing violence every day: How we are harmed, how we can heal.* Penguin Group.

W3C. (2023). Web content accessibility guidelines. https://www.w3.org/TR/WCAG21/

3

e-Poetry Framework: The Power of Choice in Digital Poetry Composition

Introduction

In this chapter, we introduce a novel approach to designing learning experiences called the e-Poetry Framework. At its core is the overlapping circles of genre, a concept that encapsulates the dynamic relationship between content creators and their audiences with the digital realm of content creation. This relationship is defined by the creator's purpose, choice of form, use of technology tools, and selection of medium and platform—all of which influence the degree of interaction, identity, and reach. Rooted in principles of backward design (Wiggins & McTighe, 2005), project-based learning (Boss & Krauss, 2022; Cooper & Murphy, 2021), and writing process approaches (Calkins, 1983; Elbow, 1998; Graves, 1983). The framework examined educator technology standards (ISTE, 2024) with composition to create a fluid connection between digital and genre-related decisions. Planning decisions encompass purpose, mode, form, audience, interaction, and permanence.

In this chapter, we explore our e-Poetry Framework, demonstrating its application as a living model in subsequent chapters (see Part II). We believe that understanding and implementing this framework is essential to humanizing digital spaces, where e-Poetry serves as a powerful medium for illuminating the potential of humanity, fostering connections through language, images, and ideas that both shape and are shaped by our world. The humanizing element of digital poetry is highlighted first by considering our students as creators in this process. In a world of machine learning, we believe a strength of our book and the framework re-centers the creation and sharing of poetry as a human process. The framework is a visual/procedural reminder that we (humans) are still in charge.

This framework is built off many layers of learning, witnessing, writing, teaching, and researching. We have received feedback on the e-Poetry Framework and continue to take this into consideration along the way to better identify how to humanize digital poetry. The framework we bring forth in this book is not linear; however, the concepts presented in this chapter are presented in the following order:

- What is the learning purpose?
- What is the mode?
- What is the form?
- Who is the audience?
- Who will interact with the content? How?
- How permanent is the artifact?

We define and explain each element of the cyclical e-Poetry Framework and then provide models for this process in Part II of this book. Each key choice is listed under the guiding questions below. Learn and process with us, then use Figure 3.2 to design your digital poetry unit.

What Is the Learning Purpose?
- Student-driven
- Teacher-driven
- Professional Learning Community (PLC)-driven
- Textbook-driven

At the heart of authentic composition is choice (see Figure 3.1). When designing units of instruction, teachers make a lot of

38 ◆ Teaching Poetry in a Digital World

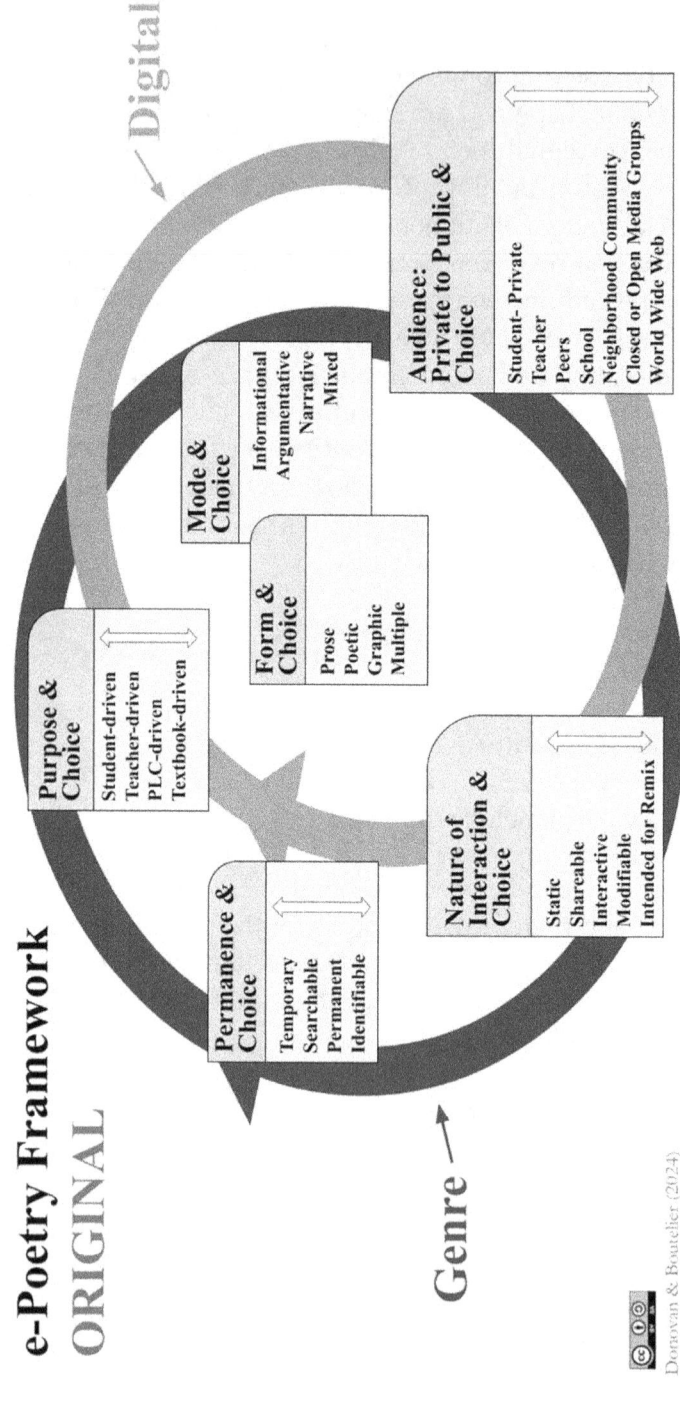

FIGURE 3.1 e-Poetry Framework: Original

decisions, and sometimes their decisions are limited because of pacing guides, textbook-driven curriculum, access to resources, and school policies. Still, there are many opportunities within the composing process where teachers can be transparent about what decisions they have made for the assignment and what decisions students can or must make. This framework attempts to show the range of decisions and how to make the e-composition process authentic: Purpose, mode, form, audience, e-interactions, and content permanence—who chooses?

The e-Poetry experience or assignment may be driven by students, teachers, a PLC, department decisions, or textbook pacing guides. Ideally, an e-Poetry project will be generated by a student's expressed need or hope to create something to share with others. For example, **students** may feel passionate about raising money to replace the volleyballs used in PE class, so they may make a digital flyer with a concrete poem in the shape of a volleyball. Another student may have an idea for students to write Where I'm From poems from the perspective of a favorite character alongside book covers to increase book checkouts at the library. In this way, teachers can design a unit or assignment that begins with students brainstorming issues that they care about, which can lead to them developing an authentic digital poetry composition. The affordance of time also impacts the purpose; do students already know how to use the form, mode, and technology (in which case it can be a brief creative experience), or the poetry and technology need detailed instruction?

The **teacher** may drive the e-Poetry work by drawing on a common formative assessment that reveals a readiness for a specific skill or content. For example, in a reading assessment, a teacher may realize students need support in inference. An e-Poetry composition may begin with a poem that describes an object but never names it and then positions the poem in a photograph where the object might live as a GIF or Meme. Students can share these on a discussion board for peers to infer the object and the clues that reveal the object. Another situation may be if there is a need to fill a segment of instructional time in between units or around special events or holidays. For example, around 9/11, one teacher curated a selection of poems: A.) "I Saw You Walking" by

Deborah Garrison (2003); B.) "When the Towers Fell" by Galway Kinnell (2008); C.) "Photography from September 11" by Wislawa Szymborska (2005); D.) "The Morning America Changed" by Stanley Plumly (2003); E.) "Going to Work" by Nancy Mercado (2010). Students silently responded to poems using the comment feature in a shared Google Doc, highlighting and responding to various lines. Then, students used a digital, collaborative whiteboard (e.g., Figma, Zoom) to create a collage of poetic lines that developed throughout the school day as each class added to the shared board/slides. This is a way of learning, witnessing, and collecting scenes without having to be confronted with graphic, visual photographs or videos.

Finally, and there may be others, the **PLC** or pacing guide of the **textbook** may drive the purpose of the e-Poetry as central or supplementary learning. While we believe in poetry integration across the curriculum and school year, some teachers and textbooks include a unit on poetry around April, during National Poetry Month. Teachers may design a unit where students create a digital chapbook of their poetry, exploring the writing of various forms and poets. A digital chapbook can be in a slide deck or digital document formatted like a book, or the digital chapbook could be a series of Instagram stories or reels, and the student's account serves as the binder or holder of the written and/or performed poems. The multimedia outcomes produce endless variations and ongoing innovations. Whether student-driven or teacher-driven, there are many more opportunities for choice that can make e-Poetry work agentive.

What Is the Mode?
- Informational
- Argumentative
- Narrative
- Mixed

In most learning standards, the modes include informational, argumentative, and narrative. The modes are deeply connected to the author's purpose, but identifying the mode is just the beginning. Writers have to make a lot of decisions about the form the writing will take in order to serve the message and reach the intended audience. In other words, when making decisions about the mode, writers also have to explore the relationship between the writer, audience, topic, and situation for the writing, including how the writing reaches the audience. Most teachers know this as "rhetorical modes." Of course, many writers/creators blend these modes when they are composing, drawing on narrative to show a situation, offering multiple sides of an issue to show balanced argumentation, and defining terms to inform readers.

Some school districts have a strict scope and sequence outlining when teachers will teach each mode, and this is usually to make sure students learn to write in each mode (year after year). However, the situation for the writing, or genre, can also vary year-to-year, and e-Poetry offers a great framework for incorporating poetry in the various modes of writing at any time. Mode and form are often parallel choices or have a relational interpretation, which is why the framework places them overlapped. We explore more of this crossover next.

What Is the Form?
- Prose
- Poetic
- Graphic
- Multiple

When integrating technology into poetry projects, understanding the form of your digital content is crucial. The form dictates how the content is presented and interacted with, influencing the overall impact and engagement with your audience. In digital spaces, content can take various forms—prose, poetic, graphic, or multiple—and each form offers distinct opportunities and considerations.

We have found **prose** to be the default form of writing in our work with teachers and schools. An informational essay, a personal narrative, an argumentative essay—teachers tend to assign these in prose or paragraph form. When your e-Poetry or writing project is presented as prose, it focuses on clear, continuous text without the traditional line breaks or stanzas associated with poetry. We call this prose poetry, which is a hybrid literary form that combines elements of prose and poetry. It is written in paragraphs rather than verse lines, as in traditional poetry, but it maintains the heightened language, imagery, and emotional intensity typical of poetry. The content of prose poetry can be as varied as traditional poetry. It can explore abstract concepts, personal reflections, or vivid descriptions, often with a strong emphasis on capturing moments, feelings, or philosophical insights (see David Ignatow's [1993] "Information," Amy Lowell's [1955] "Bath," and Harryette Mullen's [2006] "Kill Bugs Dead"). Here is an example from JustYA (2024), a young adult anthology of short poems, fiction, and essays. Notice the poetic qualities but the form as prose or paragraph:

Haibun: My Girlfriend's House by Laura Shovan (2024)

The first time I have dinner with her family, it's chaos. She has too many brothers and I have none. Her father is a megaphone—blasting jokes, opinions, questions over beef stew. *What do your parents do? What are young going to study in college? Play any sports?* There are six of us at the table, everyone's hands reaching and grabbing. *You had two rolls already, that's mine!* Only her mother is calm, spooning stew into her mouth. She speaks underneath the noise: *Why don't you two go for a walk? The boys will clear up.* The uproar! They're still complaining as we slip out the door. There's an abandoned house my girlfriend wants to show me. She takes my hand, leads me to twin tire tracks through the woods. The sun is setting on the mossy house. She points to the yellow paint and white curtains printed with flowers. *Someone lived here,* she says. *Someone cared about this place.* But to me, the house is like a pat of butter, melting, and the woods are hungry for something to tear apart.

Beware of Dog sign
fused to tree trunk's thick bark
silent forest

Poetic forms such as the haiku, two-voices, zip-ode, pile, and nonet featured in this book retain the structural elements of poetry, such as line breaks, stanzas, and rhythm. When e-Poetry is presented in a poetic form, it maintains its artistic qualities and adheres to traditional or experimental poetic structures. This form is ideal for projects that aim to showcase the beauty of language and the playfulness of poetic techniques. Digital platforms can enhance poetic forms with multimedia elements, such as interactive annotations or visual representations, that complement the textual content.

Graphic forms involve visual elements that complement or convey the content. e-Poetry or projects presented in a graphic form might include images, infographics, or other visual elements that enhance the text or provide additional context. For example, a poem could be paired with illustrations or designed as a graphic poster. This form can make the content more engaging and accessible, especially for visual learners, but it also requires attention to how the visuals and text work together cohesively.

Multiple forms integrate various types of content into a unified project. This might include combinations of prose, poetry, graphics, and interactive elements. For example, a digital project could feature a poem accompanied by a video, audio recording, and interactive commentary sections. The multiple forms approach allows for a rich, multidimensional experience but also necessitates careful planning to ensure that all elements contribute effectively to the overall message and experience. Here is where multimodality for design, as discussed in Chapter 2, comes in (e.g., "Standard 7, Multimodal Literacies" Students will comprehend and communicate knowledge through alphabetic, aural, visual, spatial, and/or gestural content" [OSDE, n.d.]). For planning purposes, teachers need to anticipate what instruction is needed to support students in creating a text (alphabetic) that lives as or with other modalities (aural, visual, spatial, and/or gestural content).

Sometimes students and teachers or PLCs will offer choices with regard to the form the mode-based writing takes. For example, the informational essay could be a pantoum. The pantoum is a poem of any length, composed of four-line stanzas in which the second and fourth lines of each stanza serve as the first and third lines of the next stanza. The last line of a pantoum is often the same as the first. One exciting aspect of the pantoum is its subtle shifts in meaning that can occur as repeated phrases are revised with different punctuation and thereby given a new context. Teachers could invite students to craft a narrative poem retelling a story written by or within a time period under study.

For example, in a Latinx literature course, students may read: "A Very Old Man with Enormous Wings" by Gabriel Garcia Marquez, "The Autumn of the Patriarch" by Gabriel Garcia Marquez, or "Get in the Halloween Spirit with 8 Bone-Chilling Stories" from Carolina Sanin, Julio Cortazar, Horacio Quiroga, Carlos Fuentes, Jorge Luis Borges, Bernardo Esquinca, and Juan Rulfo. So, the narrative poem would include five stanzas: Exposition, rising action, climax, denouement, and resolution. See Anna's Poem, "Circuits," in response to *The Circuit* by Francisco Jimenez (Roseboro, 2019):

"This is real," he thought, raising a wire of steel.
To survive, his family had to steal.
No! not food. No! Steal across the border
Just to get a job. "This is real".

Season by season he was packed up to ride
Squished between brothers, side by side
To pick cotton, strawberries, and grapes when in season.
Arriving late, leaving early, missing school. That's the reason
They called it working the circuit.

The circuit of the sun, from sun-up to sun-down.
The circuit of the crops – up north; down south, all around.
Attending school when and where he could.
He'd work hard to succeed. Yes, he would.

At school they mostly spoke English, but why?
Spanish is easier. Who can deny?
But English is what he had to learn
And the midnight oil he had to burn.

And this he did from season to season.
And that's the reason
He's a professor today, showing the way,
Having learned, the what and the why.
Following the circuit, learning the lessons.
Showing that you, too, can make it if you try.

The cognitive demand of synthesizing a novel into five stanzas takes such precision in selecting key ideas to concisely and powerfully convey meaning. The poetry can be converted to prose or paragraph form, but will it be any more accurate or meaningful with more words?

By considering form and being intentional about form in planning, you can tailor your e-Poetry and digital projects to fit the goals of your lesson and the needs of your students. Understanding the form helps make informed decisions about how to present content, engage audiences, and utilize digital tools effectively. Encourage students to experiment with these forms and to think about how their chosen format enhances their message and interaction with their audience. This awareness not only enriches their creative process but also equips them with skills for effective digital communication in their future endeavors.

Who Is the Audience?
- Student Private
- Teacher
- Peers
- School
- Neighborhood Community
- Closed or Open Media Groups
- World Wide Web

What the teacher or students do with the poetry depends on the audience, and often, this is where the assignment stops. Students turn in their work for a grade; the audience is the teacher. The poem is a linear e-Poetry, digital text perhaps to make it easy to submit on the learning management system (LMS) to be scored by a rubric (Dalton & Proctor, 2014). However, we think there is a range of considerations for teachers and students, and, at minimum, we think it is important to make this part really clear to students and even include it in the assignment or unit design intentionally to make the most of the digital potential of technology in composition.

When guiding students in creating e-Poetry, one of the most critical aspects to consider is the intended audience. This decision significantly impacts the content, form, and purpose of their work. Hopefully, you are beginning to see why we have circles within the e-Poetry Framework related to genre (mode, form, purpose) and technology (audience, interaction, permanence) (revisit Figure 3.1).

As teachers, it's essential to help students understand early in the writing process who will be viewing or engaging with their poetry, as this awareness will shape their approach to writing and sharing their work. Privacy issues are paramount; students need to be clear about who will see their poem before they begin crafting it, as this will influence their level of disclosure and vulnerability.

The audience for e-Poetry can vary widely, from **private** notebooks to **public** platforms. If the poem is intended for private reflection, it may reside in a secured digital file or a physical notebook. In this case, the poem remains a personal exploration and is not subjected to external critique or exposure. Conversely, if the e-Poetry is to be shared with a **teacher, peers,** or a broader audience, the approach and content will differ significantly. For instance, a poem shared for a classroom assignment might be submitted through an LMS for grading, while a poem intended for peer review might be posted on a discussion board where classmates can read and comment.

When considering a wider audience, such as the **school or neighborhood community,** it's crucial to think about how the content will be disseminated. Will the poem be displayed on hallway TVs, shared on the school's Facebook page, or perhaps featured in a local gallery or museum? Each medium has its own set of considerations for accessibility and impact. For example, if a poem is displayed on a school's public website, it can reach a broader audience but also requires careful consideration of privacy and appropriateness.

The choice of platform—whether it's a **closed** media group, an **open** social media account, or a **global web** presence—affects how the poem is perceived and interacted with. Students and educators need to be aware of who can view, comment on, and share their work. Understanding the extent of interaction and the potential reach of their content helps them make informed decisions about how to present their poetry. For example, a poem shared on an open Instagram account might attract comments from strangers, whereas one posted on a private Google Doc will remain confined to a select audience.

Planning ahead is crucial for making the most of digital opportunities in composition. Teachers should incorporate audience considerations into the assignment design, explicitly stating who the intended readers are and how the content will be shared. This foresight helps students align their creative choices with the purpose of their work, whether it's to entertain, inform, persuade, or connect with others. By addressing these factors, students can create meaningful e-Poetry that resonates with their intended audience while navigating the complexities of digital privacy and publication.

Who Will Interact with the Content? How?
- Static
- Interactive
- Shareable
- Modifiable
- Intended for Remix

When incorporating technology into poetry projects, it's essential to consider how your content will interact with digital spaces. Digital poetry can be static, interactive, shareable, modifiable, or even intended for remixing, and each aspect influences how the work is experienced and perceived.

If the e-Poetry is **static**, it means it is designed to remain unchanged and is meant to be read in its original form. This approach works well when you want to present a finished piece that stands on its own without encouraging further interaction or modification. For instance, a poem published in a school digital newsletter is static; it is intended to be read and appreciated as it is. Of course, people may read the print version and have conversations with one another or even the author, but the digital art content is static and not designed for digital interaction.

However, if your project involves **interaction**, it invites commentary or engagement from the audience. Interactive e-Poetry might be hosted on platforms that allow readers to leave feedback or engage in discussions. This form encourages dialogue and can enrich the reader's experience, but it also means that the content may evolve through these interactions. If the school newsletter is digital, there may be a comment tool embedded in the website, and this makes the content interactive digitally.

When content is **shareable**, it is designed to be disseminated beyond the original context. Shareable e-Poetry, like a poem shared on social media platforms, can reach a wider audience and may include interactive elements such as likes, shares, or comments. This dynamic quality can amplify the poem's impact but also introduces the possibility of it being modified, critiqued, or remixed by others.

Modifiable content allows for changes and adaptations by the audience. If a poem is shared in a Google Doc, for example, others might take the text and set it to video or images, creating a new version of the work. This ability to modify and remix means that the original content can be transformed, leading to new interpretations and interactions. It is crucial for creators to consider how their work might be altered and provide clear attribution or a link back to the original content to maintain a connection to the source.

Finally, if the e-Poetry is **intended for remix,** it invites others to creatively engage with the original work, often resulting in something entirely new. For example, a poem might be created for the purpose of being remixed with music and moving images, changing its mode, form, and audience. This creative process can enhance the poem's reach and impact but requires awareness of how the new versions relate to the original work and how they are credited.

Awareness of these aspects—static, interactive, shareable, modifiable, and intended for remix—is crucial for students and teachers alike. By understanding and guiding these interactive qualities, you help students navigate the implications of their digital footprint and make informed decisions about how they share and present their work. Consider whether the work should remain personal and intimate or explore public possibilities, and ensure that these conversations are transferable to students' future digital engagements. This approach not only enriches their learning experience but also prepares them for meaningful and ethical participation in the digital world.

There are so many considerations in this realm. For example, if a student shares a poem on a Google Doc, another person may take the text of the poem and set it to a video of images and music. There is now a need to show the trail to the original content. The text of the poem may stay the same, but with music and moving images (also published on a different platform), the mode, form, audience, and nature of interaction have all changed. If the poem is in a school digital newsletter, the poem may be intended to be read by the school. If it is a poem next to a photograph shared as a story on Instagram, then sharing and comments are likely expected. If it is on a reel, it may want a remix with music and other pictures, texts, and stickers. The extent to which the creator can control the engagements changes depending on whether the digital poem is in a space where the audience can interact, share, and/or modify the content. Revisit Chapter 2 to consider peer-fair use when remixing.

We emphasize that awareness of the audience and the interactive qualities of composition in digital spaces are essential learning opportunities. Teachers need to support students in making decisions about the implications of technifying their writing and the short and long-term footprint of that work. Always question if the student and content are served more authentically and ethically by keeping it intimate—personal for them, or classroom only—or by exploring public possibilities. Be intentional that the conversations we are having about e-Poetry are transferable to students beyond the classroom and into their futures.

How Permanent Is the Artifact?
- Temporary
- Searchable
- Permanent
- Identifiable

When integrating technology and social media into your classroom projects, particularly with poetry and other student-generated content, it's essential to consider how your work will live in digital spaces. As you design these projects, one critical question to ask is: How will this artifact live in the worlds our students engage in—school, social media, community, and the World Wide Web broadly? Understanding the nature of digital permanence can help you make informed decisions that balance the benefits of public sharing with the necessary considerations for safety and ethics, which we discussed in Chapter 2 on digital citizenship.

First, consider the **temporary** nature of the content. Digital tools within a secure school environment, like an LMS, often provide a controlled space where content is accessible only to the intended audience. This can be beneficial for projects intended to remain within the educational context. However, for projects that go public on platforms like YouTube or Google Sites, the content can be accessed far beyond the school community. Here, you must weigh the advantages of extending the reach of a message against potential risks to privacy and safety. Publicly shared content can be seen by students, families, and even strangers, which brings both opportunities for broader impact and concerns about exposure.

Next, think about the **searchability** of your content. Once something is published online, it can often be found through search engines. This searchability means that content intended to be ephemeral might outlive its expected duration. For instance, a video or blog post might remain accessible even if you no longer want it to be. Consider the implications of this searchability on students' privacy and the potential for their work to be used or misinterpreted outside the classroom.

Permanence is another crucial factor. Determine how long the artifact needs to be accessible and the implications if the

URL changes, the platform shuts down, or the content is deleted. If you use platforms that might not be permanent, consider whether there will be a hard copy or an alternative way to preserve the content. This ensures that even if the digital version becomes inaccessible, there is still a record of the student's work.

Finally, consider **identifiability**. Will the author or contributors be identifiable, and for how long? Ensure that student privacy is protected and that any identifiable information is handled with care. This consideration is vital to protect students' personal information and to adhere to school policies.

By addressing these aspects thoughtfully, you can create a digital environment where students feel both empowered and secure. Embrace the joy of integrating technology while staying informed about how your digital decisions affect your students' work and well-being.

Reflection

In this chapter, we have introduced the e-Poetry Framework that will guide the following chapters. In the next chapter, we take some time to consider how the writing process works within this framework, but here, we are offering critical considerations in the unit planning process, surfacing the many choices teachers, students, and broader learning communities can make in content creation. There can be a lot of agency and autonomy depending on how you work through the framework (see Figure 3.2 to design with it). The choices are not neutral. We'd like to emphasize that this intentional planning is what humanizes technology because we are considering the human creating and the human consuming. The care you take with these decisions is a way of taking care of our communities because what we make together will have an impact on their lives.

At the heart of this process is the principle of choice—both for the teacher in designing the assignment and for the students in their creative expression. When designing e-Poetry units, teachers have a range of decisions to make, from the purpose of the project to the mode, form, and audience. The purpose of the e-Poetry project might be driven by various factors: Students'

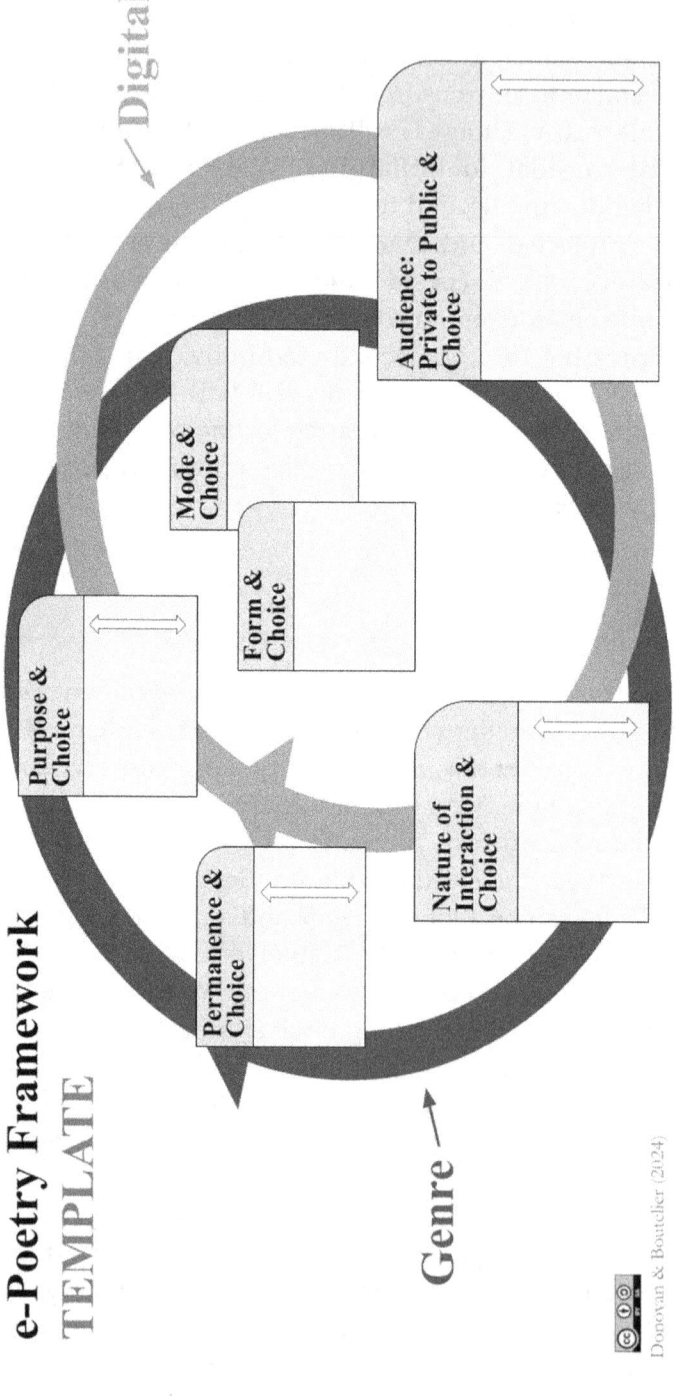

FIGURE 3.2 e-Poetry Framework template (access at bit.ly/epoetrytemplate)

interests and needs, the teacher's observations of student progress, or curriculum requirements set by a PLC or textbook pacing guide. Ideally, the project begins with students' own ideas and passions, allowing them to create content that is meaningful and relevant to them. For instance, students might use digital tools to craft poems that address local issues or personal experiences, integrating their work into a broader digital community through platforms like Instagram or a class website.

The mode and form of the e-Poetry—whether informational, argumentative, narrative, or a blend—also play a crucial role. Teachers can encourage students to experiment with different forms, such as prose poetry, graphic poetry, or multimedia projects. This exploration helps students understand how different formats can enhance their message and engage their audience. For example, a narrative poem could be paired with digital illustrations or set to music, creating a multi-layered experience that resonates on multiple levels.

Audience considerations further shape the project. Whether the e-Poetry is intended for private reflection, classroom sharing, or public dissemination, understanding the audience impacts the content, form, and delivery of the work. Teachers should guide students in considering how their poetry will be received, whether by peers, the school community, or a wider audience online. This awareness fosters a more deliberate approach to content creation and sharing, helping students navigate issues of privacy, impact, and digital footprint.

By making these decisions transparent and providing opportunities for student agency, teachers can create a humanizing experience that respects and amplifies the voices of the students. This approach not only enhances the learning process but also ensures that technology is used thoughtfully, supporting both the creation and consumption of content in ways that are impactful and respectful.

Reference List

Boss, S., & Krauss, J. (2022). *Reinventing project-based learning: Your field guide to real-world projects in the digital age.* International Society for Technology in Education.

Calkins, L. (1983). *Lesson from a child: On the teaching and learning of writing.* Heinemann.

Cooper, R., & Murphy, E. M. (2021). *Project based learning: Real questions, real answers, how to unpack PBL and inquiry.* Times 10 Publications.

Dalton, B., & Proctor, C. P. (2014). The changing landscape of text and comprehension in the age of new literacies. In J. Coiro, M. Knobel, C. Lankshear, & D. J. Leu (Eds.), *Handbook of research on new literacies* (pp. 297–324). Routledge.

Elbow, P. (1998). *Writing without teachers.* Oxford University Press.

Garrison, D. (2003). I saw you walking. *The New Yorker*, 68. https://www.newyorker.com/magazine/2001/10/22/i-saw-you-walking

Graves, D. (1983). *Writing: Teachers and children at work.* Heinemann.

Ignatow, D. (1993). Information. In *Against the evidence: Selected poems 1934–1994.* Wesleyan University Press.

International Society for Technology in Education. (2024). *ISTE educator standards.* ISTE. https://iste.org/standards/educators

Kinnell, G. (2008). When the towers fell. In *Strong is your hold: Poems.* Houghton Mifflin Harcourt.

Lowell, A. (1955). Bath. In *The complete poetical works of Amy Lowell.* Houghton Mifflin Company.

Mercado, N. (2010). Going to work. *Black Renaissance/Renaissance Noire, 10*(2–3), 125–126.

Mullen, H. (2006). [Kills bugs dead]. In *Recyclopedia.* Graywolf Press.

Oklahoma State Department of Education. (n.d.). Oklahoma academic standards for English language arts: Standard 7 (3rd draft). OSDE. https://sde.ok.gov/sites/ok.gov.sde/files/documents/files/3rddraftstandard7.pdf

Plumly, S. (2003). The morning America changed. *Valparaiso Poetry Review, IV,* I.

Roseboro, A. (2019). Circuits. *Ethical ELA.* https://www.ethicalela.com/september-1-5-day-writing-challenge/

Shovan, L. (2024). Haibun: My girlfriend's house. In S. Donovan (Ed.), *Just YA: Short poems, fiction, & essays for grades 7–12* (p. 78). Oklahoma State University Libraries. Ethical ELA.

Szymborska, W. (2005). Photograph from September 11. In *Monologue of a dog: New poems*, 69. Houghton Mifflin Harcourt.

Wiggins, G. P., & McTighe, J. (2005). *Understanding by design.* ASCD.

4

From Draft to Digital: Understanding Writing Process Approaches to Poetry and Technology

Have you ever been frustrated with the writing your students turned in? Maybe you asked your students to respond to a question expecting a paragraph or even an essay, but all you get are sentence fragments or an informal, sometimes a passive retort stating the obvious. Or maybe you designed a great project with tons of room for students to be creative and a full week to do it on their own, but you received a series of uninspiring slide decks submitted at 11:59 pm the night it's due. Or maybe you've been disappointed by the writing students submitted for their personal essays. It is about them, after all. You were hoping for something engaging, maybe even moving, certainly a couple of pages worth, but after spreading one class period's papers of paragraphs, it occurs to you that your instructions may have been the problem.

Of course, it is possible that your students waited until the last minute. Their fragments and "IDKs" implied doubt about the content or uncertainty about expectations. Their lack of inspiration may have been due to a busy weekend, but it could have been because they didn't work through a writing process. You might be seeing their very first draft. We believe that the first draft is really important and that sometimes, the first draft is all that students may do if they are exploring a topic or trying out an idea. However, if you want students to really learn something, to synthesize their learning (and writing), to come to new discoveries about what they know, how they know it, and what and how they want to share that with others, they are going to need time to work through a writing process. We can almost guarantee that the product they submit will be some of their best work that you will enjoy assessing and grading.

If you are familiar with the writing process theory, you can skip this section of the book. We offer the next few pages as a brief introduction to the writing process pedagogy and include some resources that we hope will be helpful as students create digital poetry.

A Writing Process

The instructional method associated with efforts to reform writing practices is the process writing approach (Atwell, 1987; Calkins, 1983; Graves, 1983). In most state English language arts (ELA) standards, there is a diagram of this process with arrows going from step to step in different directions because the process varies depending on the writer and writing occasion. Although there is no single definition for the process approach to writing, there are a number of common components (e.g., Graham & Perin, 2007; Nagin, 2006; Pritchard & Honeycutt, 2006). According to Graham and Sandmel (2011):

> Students engage in cycles of planning (setting goals, generating ideas, organizing ideas), translating (putting a writing plan into action), and reviewing (evaluating, editing, revising). They write for real purposes and audiences, with some of their writing projects occurring over an extended period of time. Students' ownership of their writing is stressed, as is self-reflection and evaluation.

Students work together collaboratively, and teachers create a supportive and nonthreatening writing environment. Personalized writing instruction is provided through minilessons, writing conferences, and teachable moments.

(p. 396)

At the heart of the writing process is that students are given time and support to plan, draft, and revise. The actual learning that happens during these activities and the degree of depth and skill in the writing is associated with quality writing by middle and secondary students (Breetvelt et al., 1996; Rijlaarsdam & Van den Bergh, 2006; Van den Bergh & Rijlaarsdam, 1996).

The teacher's role in the writing process is essential. By modeling the process, selecting exemplary mentor texts, guiding students through uncovering the author's decisions, and leading mini-lessons and conferences, students' writing and how they feel about writing are greatly improved. Students' motivation for writing improves as they see what they can do with time and support and as they learn to collaborate with peers in a positive, creative learning environment.

Drawing on our own experiences, we offer you this basic overview of a writing process and encourage you to revise it according to your own experiences and school models (Figure 4.1).

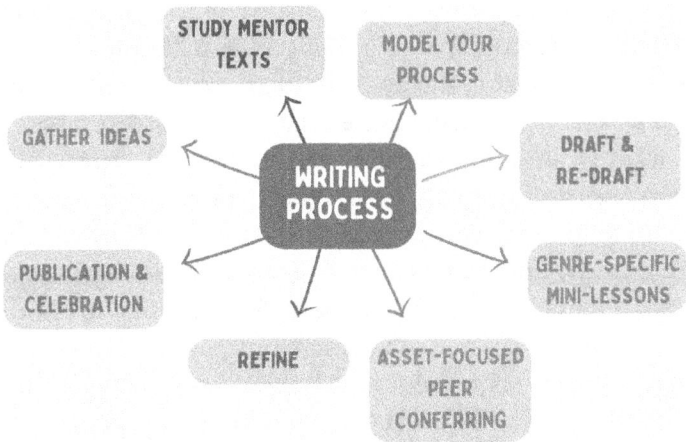

FIGURE 4.1 Writing Process. Image created by the author.

Gather Ideas

Depending on your unit and how you use the e-Poetry Framework (see Chapter 3), students will need time to decide on the topic for their writing. This works best when they can gather a number of options and do some flash writing about what they want to explore and why. For example, in the zip-ode chapter (see Chapter 6), students were studying the Armenian Genocide of 1915. The unit explored several contemporary efforts to revive and start new Armenian traditions. Students were invited to research one of several efforts, such as youth carpet weaving and tourism. For the haiku GIF chapter (see Chapter 5), students wrote poetry about art hung in the hallways of the school, so students walked around the school gathering potential ideas. They took notes and did some flash drafting before choosing which poem they wanted to make into a GIF.

Study Mentor Texts

For poetry and technology, we recommend that teachers and students find many examples or mentor texts to show how these artifacts actually live in the world. In other words, what are some great examples of the poem and the media? Maybe teachers cannot find examples of the poem and technology we offer here—because we are trying to innovate—but there are examples of poetry and examples of the media. Studying mentor texts means taking class time to look at these and, together, create a list of criteria that make them effective or good. In doing this, you also illuminate variances and possibilities in students making their own. This all means that you and your students will have a very clear idea of the assignment expectation while understanding the authentic purpose of these texts. We like posting examples of craftful poetry and media in the classroom to remind students of the mentor texts they can borrow from or modify. Imitation is a writing strategy for inspiration here and not plagiarism—model and share this concept with students.

We recommend that you reach out to your librarian and colleagues for favorite mentor texts. We hope you will look to Ethical ELA (www.ethicalela.com) for the many poetry mentor texts, including *Just YA*, an Open Education Resource of over 100 mentor texts (Donovan, 2024).

Model Your Own Process

Before or while students start drafting their poems or creating their media, a key principle of the writing process is for the teacher to create with students. There are so many instructional opportunities for a teacher to talk through a draft of a poem, show how to problem solve, or candidly say when they are stuck. In writing a zip-ode for the first time, Sarah struggled to find symbols for the zeros (see Chapter 6), and she talked through this. A student suggested she Google symbols, and this inquiry led to some great options for the poem. We can attest to the challenges of writing with students—we both get very anxious about it. Still, we find this to be the best instruction for us because we can step into students' shoes—we are all learners.

Make Time to Draft and Re-Draft

As the teacher drafts a poem or models the creation of a GIF or YouTube short, students also need time to do this. Create class time for students to get started while you walk around and check in on them to see who needs support. This is a great assessment tool, too. When teachers can watch students write, they can see what additional or modified instruction students need. Furthermore, teachers can circle back to modeling a strategy or finding new mentor texts so students can draw on those resources.

Teach Genre-Specific Mini-Lessons

We will unpack this word genre a bit more below, but genre-specific mini-lessons are not likely a term you've seen in writing process graphics. What we mean by genre-specific is that you want to teach specific moves you expect to see in your students' work. And you will likely only assess or grade the skills you teach. For example, in the spoken word two-voices poem chapter, Sarah will teach ethos, pathos, and logos because spoken word is a genre that typically moves listeners to some understanding or action about an issue. In that chapter, you will see Sarah studying mentor texts for their ethos, pathos, and logos and then asking students to identify these things in their poetry. In another genre, like haiku GIF, animation is a key feature, so we'd do a mini-lesson about how to create meaningful animations.

Facilitate Asset-Focused Peer Conferring

After students have a draft of their poem and/or a draft of their e-Poetry (poem with the technology), we recommend students do some peer conferring. Peer conferring is very different from peer editing or revising. We do not think peers should be "correcting" one another's work, but rather, we believe peers are an authentic audience who can tell the creator their honest experiences with content. The peer can ask to do a mirror-point-wonder (M-P-W) conference (see Table 4.1). This protocol was inspired by Elbow (1998), who said that what writers need more than anything is to know how their audience experiences their work. The peer will mirror back what they heard, saw, felt, and experienced. Then, the peer will point to what craft move or effect had that impact. Finally, the peer will wonder or post questions for the creator to offer time and space for the creator to reflect on the next steps. After both peers confer, the students work on revisions informed by the feedback, poem mentor texts, and technology mentors, drawing on all they learned to refine their artifacts.

Make Time to Refine and Reflect

After every draft or every sharing, a writer-creator needs an opportunity to refine their work. This may mean reordering, deleting, adding, or modifying something. Ideally, this is informed by the criteria the class illuminated by studying mentor texts. We include rubrics at the end of each chapter with some basic criteria we look for in our e-Poetry creations. As you try out each of these poems and media, you will see how you might want to refine your project for hours and hours. It may never feel done, but you will decide when the project is due. For example, when Stefani was creating the haiku GIF example, she kept playing with the color of the font and the timing of the phrases (the animation).

We created this simple rubric to reflect an assessment of the writing process. This aligns with most state standards and includes an additional element: The Artist Statement.

Not every student (or teacher) is going to be able to completely refine their poetry or digital creation to the same aesthetic standard, and there will always be technical skills that need more time than we have to develop. In the writing process classroom,

TABLE 4.1 Peer Conferring Protocol

1. Peer begins by **asking questions**:
    a. *Tell me about this piece, such as the mode, genre, or what you are going for.*
    b. *Is there some part in particular you'd like me to notice or attend to?*
    c. *Please read it to me.*
2. Writer **reads aloud** with a pencil or access to the digital copy to revise in the moment. In reading aloud, writers hear and notice line-level needs and easy copy edits.
3. Peer **listens**.
    - In an early draft or final draft, the peer listens to be a mirror for their partner—reflecting back what they understand and/or how it fits with the mode/genre. This may mean beautiful phrases and subjects explored. This may mean authentic dialogue or vivid word choice, but it may just mean witnessing some aspect of their classmate's life or writing identity (being present).
    - However, if the peer is listening for line or word level issues (or use of white space), then the peer will **look** at the text, which is most useful in poetry and multimodal pieces that depend on headers and figures. We expect the writer to read with a pencil or access their digital copy to make live edits or revisions as they may notice spots in need of attention.
4. After the read-aloud, the peer **responds, M-P-W**:
    - **Mirror**: *So, from what I heard, this piece is making me consider/feel/remember ....*
    - **Point**: *When you read...I found that line to be especially vivid/convincing/moving/curious...Your overall theme (e.g., the author's comment about humanity) seems to be....because...Is that what you intended?*
    - **Wonder**: *Now, here's what I am wondering:* Tell me more about your inspiration for this piece...What might another point of view add to this... Tell me about the sources for the quotes....why these? Tell me about why the character reacted this way...Tell me about the part where...what was your intention? Tell me about this metaphor...Tell me more about how you decide to begin (or end). Tell me about this claim or that evidence—how do you see those connected?
5. Writer adds notes into a comment box of the document or in a notebook and makes revisions then or later.

(Switch writer and peer roles).

we celebrate growth, so we offer here, as part of the refinement stage, an opportunity for students to write about their process, which shows their content knowledge and skill development as well as their understanding of the mentor texts, genre, and mini-lessons. Let's look at the haiku GIF rubric in Chapter 5 (see Table 4.2). The first criterion is that they submitted a final artifact. Then, there is an assessment of the poetry craft and then

TABLE 4.2 Example Rubric: Haiku GIF

	Haiku GIF Rubric and Artist Statement
Assignment Component	*Meet Expectations (2 pts)*
Final e-Poetry Submission	You submitted a complete, polished poetry artifact. In this final piece, you considered peer and facilitator feedback and carefully edited the piece for form, style, grammar, language, technology, etc.
Poetry Craft Moves Standard: Write informative/ explanatory texts to examine and convey complex ideas, concepts, and information clearly and accurately through the effective selection, organization, and analysis of content.	Informational Haiku • 3 lines • Meter 5-7-5 • Shift, or the turn to the third line, is reflective of an aha about the subject
Technology Component Standard: Use technology, including the Internet, to produce and publish writing and to interact and collaborate with others.	GIF • Color(s) is symbolic or thematic • Symbolic objects (one or two) • Movement (animation of the image/text) that is meaningful or relevant to the shift (aha) in the poem with timing aligned • File .gif
1 Revision Strategy	The final piece and/or artist statement demonstrates that at least one revision strategy from the course was attempted. (A writer may choose not to use a revision but trying it out is an important part of the process.)
Artist Statement	Your artist statement discusses how X informed your written piece, identifies the craft moves and revision strategy you implemented, describes a significant aspect of your writing process or experience, and describes what you learned as a writer from this process.

Scoring Scale:

Meets Expectations (2 pts): Thoughtfully completed in a way that reflects course lessons and meets criteria.

Partially Developed (1): The product is only partially developed, or it reflects course lessons in a limited way. Revisit course activities and lessons or instructor feedback for further development.

Missing/Incomplete (0): The assignment is missing or incomplete to a degree that it is not able to be scored. Or the artifact does not reflect the assignment guidelines.

(Continued)

TABLE 4.2 *(Continued)*

Haiku GIF Rubric and Artist Statement

Artist Statement (handout offered during class)

- What surprised you about (topic) while you were crafting the project? Give a specific example. (For example... For instance...) What successes resulted from the project?
- Tell us about your process—how did you get from beginning to end in writing this piece?
- Which mentor texts had the biggest impact on your thinking and writing? (Name the author/colleague, name the text, or explain how you used the mentor texts to inspire your writing)
- Which craft elements and/or mini-lessons impacted the revision and meaning of your writing?
- Which peer feedback influenced your choices; please cite classmates?
- What did you learn about the topic/context/subject of this piece that you may not have known or understood when you first began writing this?
- What do you understand about this mode and genre in particular that you may not have known or understood when you first began
- What did you learn about yourself as a writer and content creator? (For example ... For instance ...)

the technology. Each is assessed differently for the skills or components you spend learning in class. Next, students show a revision strategy: This can be something the teacher suggested or showed in a genre-specific mini-lesson or something a peer suggested during the peer conferring. And then finally, the student-creator writes a reflection about the process. Sarah usually invites students to select three prompts from the list to write about. This artist statement is a metacognitive step in refining student thinking and understanding of their writing process (see Box 4.1). For Sarah, this is one of her favorite pieces of writing to read because it shows a depth of learning with very personal insights.

Box 4.1

Teacher poet tip: You might also write your own artist statement to reflect on the digital poetry lesson you facilitated or the poetry you composed

At the end of each chapter in Part II, we will share a sample rubric like the one below with slight variations for each poem and technology.

Publish and Celebrate

Depending on the e-Poetry Framework decisions, you will decide how to publish the student work. It may be class-wide, grade-wide, school-wide, community-wide, or totally public. As discussed in Chapter 2, be sure you follow your district's digital policies. Still, publishing is a big deal. We recommend that, instead of making a dramatic due date that might strike fear or nervousness, you frame the publication as a party or celebration. Sarah would call the due date the "Publication Party." For the party, students would go live with their project in a countdown, and then Sarah would pass around cookies while students read, viewed, and commented on one another's projects. Sarah would model how to write asset-based celebratory feedback using her celebratory three-response framework (see Table 4.3), and then students would respond to one another throughout the class period while enjoying their cookies. For more public publications, you can arrange for community members to write comments, or have a gallery at a local library, or send an email to parents that a project is live on the school website or school Facebook page. Engage students in planning the publication party, as they will have great ideas.

A Word About Genre

After traversing middle, secondary, and college writing worlds over the past few years, we now realize that we have conflated and confused writing terminology in our instruction. The way the standards or objectives are written for writing typically frame writing by categories (e.g., narrative, informational, and argument in grades 3 through 12), which then leads to assignments also framed around such categories.

Many school districts' ELA curriculum guides might include a narrative unit in the first quarter, an informational unit in the

TABLE 4.3 Complimenting Writers

Complimenting Writers	From the Heart (Pathos)	From the Mind (Logos)	From the Writer in Me (Ethos)
Instruction	Respond by sharing a memory that surfaced for you. Did you have a similar experience? Did this remind you of something from your life?	What did the writer say that you liked, learned from, or never considered before this moment? Did you like the way the writer pointed out (something)?	What did you like about how it was written? Sound: Rhyme, repeating lines, alliteration. Pace: Short phrases, long phrases, one word. Imagery: A verb, image, pun, simile, metaphor, sensory detail (color, texture or objects).
Example Phrases	• "I can relate to the phrase '…' because…" • "When you wrote '…', I felt/was reminded… because…" • "Your words '…' really moved me/resonated with me because …"	• "The phrase '…' got me thinking about … because …" • "Until I read/heard your words '…', I had not considered … in this way. Now I see …" • "I see or understand … in a new way after reading … because…" • "I think the heart of this piece is in the line '…' because …"	• "I noticed you used the technique of … in the phrase/stanza …; its effect is…" • "A vivid word is … because …" • "A clever line is … because …" • "Your use of … gives the effect …"

Source: Donovan (2015).

second quarter, and an argumentative unit in the third quarter, with a little push for all three leading into state testing season in the fourth quarter.

Naming writing by modes makes for concrete, measurable ways of assigning and assessing the choices and moves writers make (or are told to make in the classroom). However, if we only name modes, we miss out on various genres of writing, including poetry forms and multimedia outcomes. Let's begin with a few working definitions of mode, genre, form, and text structure. Like the *writing process*, there is a range of definitions, but there are some basic principles to each of these terms (see Table 4.4).

TABLE 4.4 Mode, Genre, form, Medium, and Text Structure Definitions

Term	Definition
Mode	The primary purpose of the text: Narrative, argument, informational
Genre	The situation in which the writer, message, and reader are interacting, and this is dynamic and responsive (Giltrow, 2002); [I]naugurals, eulogies, courtroom speeches, and the like have conventional forms because they arise in situations with similar structures and elements (Miller, 2015)
Form	How communication appears on the page or screen (visual and spatial modalities); its physical blocks of information: Paragraphs, stanzas, lists, tables, images, sound, video (visual, audio, aural and gestural modalities)
Medium	Refers to the method or material used to create and present content, e.g., envelope, paper letter, text message, cereal box
Text structure	Refers to how the text ideas are organized: Chronological, compare/contrast, problem-solution, cause-effect, how-to, non-linear

Genre helps us put a name on what we are reading and writing—a way of talking about the text and how the text lives in the world. What *genre* means in literature (e.g., poetry, drama or biography, mystery) is not quite the same as *genre* in writing (e.g., news article, speech, lab report, college application essay).

When I (Sarah) was visiting my six-year-old niece, she wanted to show me a picture of a dilophosaurus in her nonfiction book. I watched as she turned to the table of contents in her dinosaur encyclopedia, scanned the page, and then turned to the dilophosaurus page. She knew and depended on the organizational structures of her informational book. This is the heart of genre: Writers typically write within the "rules" of a genre for a specific audience, expecting those rules when they approach the text. If there is something unexpected, the readers may be frustrated or pleasantly surprised by an innovative shift in the genre. And that is another part of genre; it shifts and evolves as writers innovate, readers demand innovation, or technology demands or makes it possible.

In literature conversations, we talk about genre all the time with little (or less) confusion. Fiction genres include realistic, mystery, science fiction, etc. Nonfiction genres include biography, memoir, diary, etc. Genres, in this sense, are categories of literature; however, does genre work the same way in writing instruction? According to Devitt (1993), when we, as readers, recognize the genre of a text:

> We make assumptions not only about the form but also about the text's purpose, its subject matter, its writer, and its expected reader. If I open an envelope and recognize a sales letter in my hand, I understand that a company will make a pitch for its product and want me to buy it. Once I recognize that genre, I will throw the letter away or scan it for the product it is selling.
>
> (p. 574)

Genre is more than purpose (modes) and medium (paper, email); it entails the rhetorical situation and the social context. When we teach genre, we aren't just teaching what form the communication will take; we are teaching about the situation in which the writer, message, and reader are interacting, and this is dynamic and responsive, which means our writing instruction must also be dynamic and responsive (Giltrow, 2002).

If we aren't using the writing process approach, or haven't before now, this will all feel very confusing because teachers might assign a personal narrative about a vacation and not also design the assignment as a genre: What is a real situation when a writer would write about a vacation? What message is worth sharing with readers? Who are the readers—young, same age, older, familiar with the vacation, unfamiliar? And what form will it take—an essay, a poem, a visual story? And what medium will it be: Paper, digital document, slideshow, audio recording? How often have we designed a writing assignment with consideration of genre?

Genres develop because they respond to situations that writers encounter repeatedly. The features of the genre develop out of response to their situations, and as situations change over time or context, the genre shifts. But Devitt (1993) asks: "Where does the 'situation' come from? (p. 577)…by selecting a genre to write in, or by beginning to write within a genre, the writer has selected the situation entailed in that genre" (p. 581).

The answer is in the situation. In this book, we are creating a number of situations or possibilities for genres to emerge and hope that you and your students will develop new iterations of these genres as you imagine how poetry and technology intersect.

As Miller (2015) explains, we have come to expect and know how to interact with various genres like inaugurals, eulogies, and courtroom speeches. These all have conventional forms because they have arisen in situations with similar elements, and the speaker/creators and their audience respond in similar ways. People learn from precedent what is appropriate and duplicate that, but people can also shape the genre to become something new.

One of the reasons, we think, poetry has been pushed to the margins of ELA classrooms or only used during National Poetry Month is because of the precedent of poetry being exclusive or maybe flowery language difficult to decipher. The effect that has had on some people is to turn away from it rather than engage with it, innovate it, and create new forms to have a new effect on other people.

As a teacher, what decisions must you make when creating a writing assignment? Do you choose the mode, topic, genre, text structure, medium, and form? Which decisions do students make? What mentor texts do you use to show students the precedent, and to what extent can students shape the genre into something new?

We hope the e-Poetry Framework will show teachers and students ways to draw on poetry and technology to imagine situations that call for new genres like the haiku GIF, zip-ode short, and another genre yet to be imagined.

Reflection

The writing classrooms across the United States are changing and have been changing for decades. From chalkboards to whiteboards to Smartboards. From a desktop to computer labs to rolling-shared iPad carts to 1:1 Chromebooks. From printed textbooks to digital sources offering up-to-the-minute publications. From blue books to consumable workbooks to tools resisting linear sequencing and welcoming real-time collaboration.

These transitions make us think about terminology and how we talk about and teach writing changes. Students need to develop a capacity to navigate multiple rhetorical and communication modes, media, and situations, and that means they have to have time and space to make choices, produce, respond, and revise in a social environment. They must learn ethical practices as creators and consumers of information. Writing pedagogy, therefore, cannot be about efficiency. The discovery is in the process.

The writing classroom has to be about our lives, and the moves we make to create content need just as much attention as the final product or outcome. This is the way we humanize our classrooms: By centering on the people creating content and the people for whom we are creating.

Reference List

Atwell, N. (1987). *In the middle: Reading, writing, and learning from adolescents*. Heinemann.

Breetvelt, I., Van den Bergh, H., & Rijlaarsdam, G. (1996). Rereading and generating and their relation to text quality: An application of multilevel analysis on writing process data. In G. Rijlaarsdam, H. Van den Bergh, & M. Couzjin (Eds.), *Theories, models and methodologies on writing research* (pp. 10–21). Amsterdam University Press.

Calkins, L. (1983). *Lesson from a child: On the teaching and learning of writing*. Heinemann.

Devitt, A. J. (1993). Generalizing about genre: New conceptions of an old concept. *College Composition & Communication, 44*(4), 573–586.

Donovan, S. (2015). 3 perspectives improve peer-to-peer response. *MiddleWeb*. https://www.middleweb.com/24473/3-perspectives-can-improve-peer-to-peer-response

Donovan, S. (Ed.) (2024). *Just YA: Short poems, fiction, & essays for grades 7–12*. Oklahoma State University Libraries. Ethical ELA.

Elbow, P. (1998). *Writing without teachers*. Oxford University Press.

Giltrow, J. (Ed.). (2002). *Academic reading: Reading and writing across the disciplines*. Broadview Press.

Graham, S., & Perin, D. (2007). A meta-analysis of writing instruction for adolescent students. *Journal of Educational Psychology, 99*, 445–476.

Graham, S., & Sandmel, K. (2011). The process writing approach: A meta-analysis. *Journal of Educational Research, 104*(6), 396–407. https://doi.org/10.1080/00220671.2010.488703

Graves, D. (1983). *Writing: Teachers and children at work*. Heinemann.

Miller, C. R. (2015). Genre as social action (1984), revisited 30 years later (2014). *Letras & Letras, 31*(3), 56–72.

Nagin, C. (2006). *Because writing matters: Improving student writing in our schools*. Jossey-Bass.

Pritchard, R. J., & Honeycutt, J. (2006). Process writing. In C. MacArthur, S. Graham, & J. Fitzgerald (Eds.), *Handbook of writing research* (pp. 275–290). Guilford.

Rijlaarsdam, G., & Van den Bergh, H. (2006). Writing process theory: A functional dynamic approach. In C. MacArthur, S. Graham, & J. Fitzgerald (Eds.), *Handbook of writing research* (pp. 41–53). Guilford.

Van den Bergh, H., & Rijlaarsdam, G. (1996). The dynamics of composing: Modeling writing process data. In C. Levy & S. Ransdell (Eds.), *The science of writing* (pp. 207–232). Erbaum.

PART II

5

Haiku in Motion: Celebrating School Community through GIF Poetry

I could feel the fever spiking. And my blood was simmering.

It was the week before spring break, and the symptoms of cabin fever among the students were spreading. They'd submitted their final portfolios—letters to parents with hyperlinks to all their learning for the past ten weeks—and with each day, one more classmate was absent (starting vacation early). Some students were staring off into space during reading time. Others were restless, even agitated, when I continued with our routines. I was reacting differently to each instance of resistance. I think I was coming down with the fever, too, but we had to get through three more days, and how we did that was up to us.

After school, I was reading the portfolio letters. In their conclusions, I asked students to tell me one word that captured their experience of the quarter and to comment on what they most enjoyed. Some of their words were *brave, discovery, perseverance,* and *fun.* The trend of what they most enjoyed was Friday story time and publication days with comments and cookies. They enjoyed the cookies, but they mostly enjoyed hearing one another's writing.

I have never been known as the "fun" teacher, but I was glad the students thought the class was fun. I wanted students to start spring break with those positive feelings, not boredom, restlessness, or agitation. Heck, I wanted to go out on a high note.

We didn't have time to write another paper, publish it, and share it, so I decided we'd write haiku. I figured we could publish, share, and eat cookies, and all would be right in the world. Still, I had to be clever about the process to keep the cabin fevers down.

Plan with the e-Poetry Framework

What Is the Learning Purpose?
This learning experience is teacher-driven. We all had spring fever and needed a short unit that would allow us some physical movement and inspiration to get us through the spring season of testing. Because this short unit was toward the end of the school year, students were familiar with informational writing as we had done a four-part blog series using various text structures (descriptive, sequence, compare-contrast, and problem-solution). We had also done some narrative writing with our daily write-ins and biographical exchange unit. Students were familiar with sensory and figurative language (Figure 5.1).

What Is the Mode?
The mode for Hallway Haiku GIFs is informational, specifically descriptive writing. Students created a series of haiku describing art and artifacts around the school's interior and exterior. See the Hallway Haiku section.

What Is the Form?
Because haiku is a form of poetry that traditionally explores the subject of nature and it is a short form that challenges students to be concise in their descriptions, haiku is a relevant form to use during spring. We chose the GIF to publish the haiku because GIFs depend on imagery, and we chose to showcase the art created by students and the school grounds by pairing the haiku

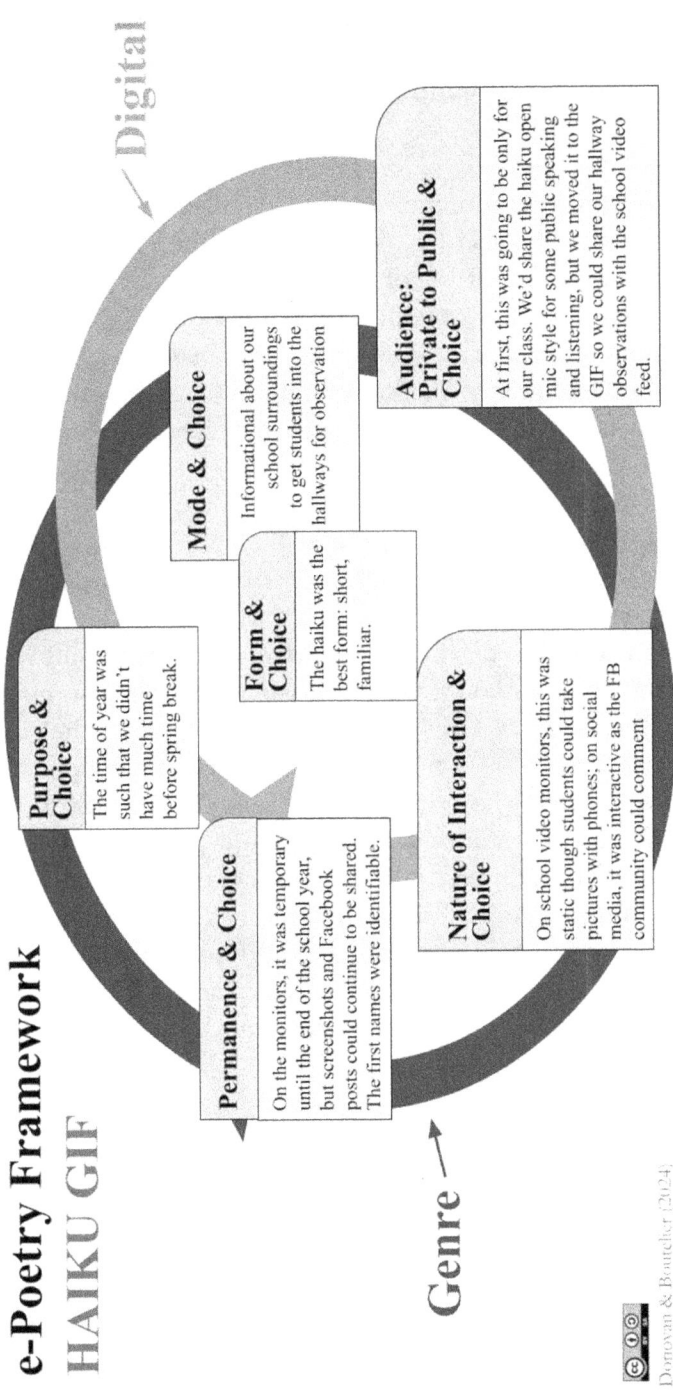

FIGURE 5.1 e-Poetry Framework: Haiku GIF

and image in a GIF. Further, GIFs show movement, and we were especially keen on moving our bodies but also showing how spring is about a time of movement and transformation.

Who Is the Audience?
For this lesson, the audience is the school community, specifically the students, faculty, staff, and visitors who walk the school hallways. The GIFs—of haiku and images of the school—were projected on our school TVs within the loop of typical announcements broadcast internally. This hallway publishing drew on our Hallway Haiku inspirations and allowed the student-poets to celebrate the artists and school artifacts that inspired their poetry.

Who Will Interact with the Content? How?
By publishing the GIFs only on the school TVs, the student work is static, meaning people can look at it and enjoy it but not necessarily interact with it digitally. Of course, students would watch the GIF and comment on it with a classmate or spend some time enjoying the series of GIFs on the TV, so there was that interaction, but the GIFs were not shared in a way that people could share, like, comment, download, or remix the GIFs. Still, there is a possibility that students would take a picture or video of the GIFs and share them on their own social media feeds. This was something we could not control but needed to consider. Like other announcements, the principal could have shared the GIFs on school social media accounts. In that case, the GIFs could be shared and interacted with, even remixed by members of the social media group.

How Permanent Is the Artifact?
The GIFs stay live on the TV screens until the end of the school year or when the video broadcaster or office announcement engineer changes the slides being projected. As for the student-poets-GIF makers, if they chose to include their name or initials, the GIF would be identifiable by the school community. As part of the publication process, students could choose whether or not or how to identify their GIFs. Further, if the principal shared

any of the GIFs on social media, then the GIF would stay in the account feed until intentionally deleted.

Learn the Poem Form: Hallway Haiku

The hallways of our school are filled with art (opportunity for discovery), so I created a gallery walk prewriting experience for students. This would get students out of their seats and maybe notice (even appreciate) the beauty of our school. However, for this to work, I could not send 32 restless, agitated students into the hallways days before spring break, so I organized stations and sent shifts of eight students at a time to do the gallery walk.

During the gallery walk, students stopped to observe different pieces (e.g., tree artwork, cell monster posters, a plaster installation, our living courtyard) and take notes using a prewriting sheet. After all the shifts had completed the gallery walk, we began crafting the poems.

By junior high, most students have written a few haiku and understand it as a three-lined poem about nature with a strict syllable count of 5-7-5. Their focus on syllables was evident as I watched students use their fingers to count or tap the beats. I liked seeing what they knew and could already do with haiku; most had mastered two of the elements of haiku: The number of syllables and the subject matter. But there's more to haiku than that, which is why teachers can nurture an understanding of haiku long into high school and beyond. Many adults are still mastering the form.

A syllable is a unit of rhythm in a spoken word consisting of one vowel, usually attached to one or more consonants. For example, "water" has two syllables. The dictionary also shows this syllabic breakdown for every word. However, with poetry, syllables are not so neat or strict. For example, "soil" in the dictionary is one syllable, but when we say it, it sure sounds like two. The same goes for chocolate and different—go with your ear or the sound you want it to be in your poem. Poetry is responsive to language in the ways we hear it and experience it—the dictionary does not have the final word: The poet does.

A traditional haiku is an unrhymed poem about nature in English written in three lines and consists of seventeen syllables exactly: 5-7-5. According to Van Den Heuvel (2000), in *The Haiku Anthology*, contemporary poets stray from these rules by experimenting with subject matter; see Regina Harris Baiocchi's *Urban Haiku* (2004), and syllables called a "liberated haiku," more concerned with the essence of haiku rather than syllables. I think junior high students are ready to consider essence since they've mastered the counting part of haiku.

Subject matter is another element of haiku. A traditional haiku focuses on nature, a concrete subject rather than an abstract concept. In other words, haiku should take place in the natural physical world and contain a seasonal word called a "kigo," placing it in one of four seasons: spring, summer, autumn, winter, and also tulips(typical in spring), baseball (takes place in summer), pumpkins (associated with fall), and snow (a sign of winter). In other words, the haiku includes a kigo to allow the reader to infer the season. A traditional haiku is set in nature in some way and a specific season.

Structure is the third part of haiku that is not often taught in the classroom. There are two parts to a haiku: Some kind of shift or movement from the beginning to end. Let's look at this example by Sarah:

> the gnarl of the sycamore's tempest-sliced phloem exposes heart scars in roots.

First, it opens with a clear sensory image (the gnarl of a tree); then the second line is a shift or movement from the image (tempest-slice or a spring storm) to an insight about the image (exposes the scars)—to a surprise, "aha," or deep personal understanding of something. The tree in the spring (or fall) storm is what makes it special. The tree separated from the storm or the storm separated from the tree is what makes it special; the context of the poem. Here is another one by Sarah:

> Looking for off switch in a harvest moon night sky—next chapter flashlight.

In this haiku, an expectation is created. You experience being a person in or outdoors at night in the fall who may be annoyed with the light from the bright harvest moon, maybe ready for sleep. It's autumn, so the air may be a little cool, and there is a feeling of sleepiness or maybe annoyance. Hold onto that feeling as your own. Have you ever been so tired, but there is light coming into your room at night or in the morning, making it difficult to rest? Next, seeing through the speaker's eyes, you are looking for a way to turn off that bright moon, but then you see the dash—the shift and embrace that extra light in the evening to read another chapter in your book. Maybe it reminds you of the days you'd read a comic or magazine with the flashlight from your phone as a child. Instead, there's a little surprise. What do you feel when you get this surprise? Remember, in the previous line, you are feeling frustrated or ready for sleep, but here, you may feel the shift in the mood to see something you didn't expect. That movement is necessary for the haiku to be alive and dynamic. If it just describes a pretty scene, it is static and lifeless because it doesn't surprise. The last line needs to be relevant to be meaningful, not random. Note: Haiku can be singular or plural. Don't add an "s" to make it plural.

When we teach students this structure of haiku, we can get them to think more deeply about the meaning of an object in a certain context; the object is special in this time, place, and situation. In a different setting, the meaning or insight would be lost, and maybe there'd be another haiku.

The next day, students revised their poems and did a peer conference to assess the structure in particular. Then, each student chose one of their four haiku to share in our class open mic style. Two students hosted the open mic, and we had a haiku fest with cookies to celebrate the end of our quarter and the beginning of spring break (Tables 5.1 and 5.2).

Before learning the technology to move the haiku into the GIF, we share the creativity of students who transformed their observations of school hallway objects within and just beyond our school into poignant haiku. These brief but powerful poems emerged from a process of mindful observation at four designated

TABLE 5.1 Hallway Haiku Observation Table

Instructions: Take this chart with you to each station and take notes in quiet observation mode, noticing different aspects of the objects according to the columns. When you return to class, write one or more haiku that capture your discoveries in that place.

Object to Observe	Allusion, Simile, Metaphor	Textures: Soft, Smooth, Rough, Crinkled, Sticky, Glossy	Thoughts: What Might It Be Thinking	Colors, Shades: Bright, Dull	Movements: How Does it Move, What Moves it	Sounds: What Sounds Does it Make	Speech/Beliefs: What Might it Say or Believe/Value	Haiku
A. Winter tree paintings, stairway upstairs by office								
B. Cell artwork by 113								
C. Kids in white sculptures by MPR								
D. Courtyard window by 126, don't go outside but look at nature								

Haiku in Motion ◆ 81

TABLE 5.2 Completed Hallway Haiku Observation Table

Object to Observe	Allusion, Simile, Metaphor	Textures: Soft, Smooth, Rough, Crinkled, Sticky, Glossy	Thoughts: What Might it Be Thinking	Colors, Shades: Bright, Dull	Movements: How Does it Move, What Moves it	Sounds: What Sounds Does it Make	Speech/Beliefs: What Might it Say or Believe/ Value
A. Winter tree paintings, stairway upstairs by office	Branches waiting for birds	Smooth and rough	Let me survive in the winter; can't wait to be covered in leaves; I feel naked with you looking at me	Dull and white, brown	by the wind it bends	Creaky branches	I want water and warmth
B. Cell artwork by 113	Allusion to humans	Smooth and rough	I must survive	Bright colors and shapes	With legs and wheels- the cells move through or are the body	Speaking to the other cells to collaborate, hash a plan	Life; cells are life
C. Kids in white sculptures by MPR	As white as snow; frozen in time	Crinkled; plastered	kids doing everyday stuff so they do not get old	White and dull; washed away	doing kid-like activities; playing arms, legs	talking and laughing	playful tone, but somber as they are frozen
D. Courtyard window by 126, don't go outside but look at nature	As colorful as a Pollack painting	Soft smooth rough	Please don't snow; can we go outside to write	Blue table, red chairs; brown grass, green trees, shadows	Wind and nature	Rustling the trees by the wind	Water, sunlight, people sitting, and using it

FIGURE 5.2 Winter tree paintings, stairway upstairs by the office (refers to Object A in Table 5.2)

stations, where students engaged their senses and applied figurative language to capture the essence of their surroundings. As you read the haiku presented in Figures 5.2–5.5, notice how the students skillfully craft imagery and language, leading to moments of insight or discovery. Each haiku serves as a testament to the students' ability to find beauty and meaning in the mundane, reflecting the unique perspectives they bring to their environment. We also highlight the importance of scaffolding and engaging with the writing process in gathering ideas before drafting.

> in the cold, white snow
> stood a lonely and bare tree
> swaying in the wind
>
> darkness everywhere
> coldness shooting down my spine
> bark keeping me warm

silent as a hawk
we wait for spring to come
but still, we hibernate

rainbows everywhere
devouring my monster
let my roar escape

green like a clover
vicious like a black mamba
ready to attack

blossoming creatures
careening all around
to find a way home

chaotic loudness
swallowed in endless plain white
aching to escape

FIGURE 5.3 Cell artwork by 113 (refers to Object B in Table 5.2)

motionless forever
in this desolate place among many
Youthful spirits in us

collective and quick
their movements go in their haste,
all going somewhere.

we're slowly blooming
rain and summer would be nice
wind crunches my leaves

FIGURE 5.4 Kids in white sculptures by MPR (refers to Object C in Table 5.2)

FIGURE 5.5 Courtyard window by 126, don't go outside but look at nature (refers to Object D in Table 5.2)

blooming and teeming
a fragment of nature herself
verdant with activity

windy day goes on
rustling branches, leaves scattered
bench waits silently

Learn the Tech: Shifting to GIF

In writing this chapter, I moved students' haiku from their papers to a Google Doc. Maybe the poems have now been moved into a paper book you are holding now. The movement of the words extends the reach of the composition to new audiences and for new purposes.

Still, it occurred to the students in the sharing of their poems during the open mic that the artists who created the artwork might want to see the poetry their work inspired. For the courtyard, we could share the poem with the school groundskeeper. For the statue, we'd have to do some research because that figure had been holding space in the hallway for decades. But for the trees and monsters, the artists were in our school, and their parents were likely on social media. What might it mean to share our poetry with the art to the artists and the community? After some brainstorming, students suggested a GIF we could project on the monitors and share on the school's social media.

As their English language arts (ELA) teacher, I had to consider how I might scaffold this part and what knowledge about the medium, including possible platforms, I'd need to know in order to support the students in the project. So, would this be a genre shift? A medium shift?

Originally, the GIF (Graphics Interchange Format) was not a genre. They are a file format for storing and displaying animated images. GIFs can be used to convey a wide range of content, from humorous and entertaining animations to informative and educational ones (Balaban & Çevik, 2020; Voigts, 2018; Zhu & Wang, 2021). They are a medium for expressing various genres, styles, and content types. However, Dirk's (2010) essay "Navigating Genres" sets some guidelines for what a genre is that might help us see how a medium becomes a genre. Genres are categorized responses to a specific and repeating social situation meant to lead to an action or another response. They have a set of expectations created from all the previous responses to that specific social situation. The modern and most popular GIF is the photographic GIFs. These looped videos of mere seconds capture the motion or reactions of people, movie or TV scenes, interviews, speeches, home videos, or actors, which are popular on social media platforms.

Like any genre, they have affordances and constraints. GIFs play automatically on a continuous loop. This allows people to view them easier and more quickly, like images, instead of having to use the interface of a video player. They're just as readily available and shareable as images. But GIFs cannot be extremely long, averaging only seconds in playtime. They aren't really an adequate method of storytelling but lend themselves to reactionary meanings. They are also silent. With no audio, creators can only use subtitles or captions to convey more meaning, like in the days of silent films. In some ways, GIFs can integrate seamlessly into people's social media feeds. As Eppink (2014) said, "It is largely because of its limitations that the GIF thrives nearly two decades after its introduction, sustaining a renewed interest in the loop" (p. 303). As an efficient multimodal form of communication—moving images with text—GIFs fulfill multiple social needs. A primary use is to convey the emotion or reaction of the GIF user to their readers. Like emojis and some text speak (e.g., lol, laughing out loud), they attempt to bring elements of face-to-face conversation to convey the tone or mood of the user, often in humorous ways.

The reactionary GIF can also be tied with specific cultural or media references that enhance the meaning or emotion for the reader. This GIF that paraphrases a line from the movie Thor both describes an opinion in a humorous way and has ties with a community that understands the context of the image.

GIFs can also be used to spread information through the use of subtitles. The informative GIFs combine compilation videos and transcripts of televised events, interviews, movies, or TV shows. Viewers can read the quote while seeing the speaker's actions.

No matter the type of GIF or its purpose, like any genre, there are GIFs that are more successful than others. The goal of turning our haiku into GIFs is to share the poetry with artists, their families, and the community and become part of the conversation around the school in the community. Of course, this is different from pop culture or political rhetoric of GIFs where we do not know the author of the GIF or art/visual media. For most GIFs, there is no obvious authorship because the creator takes a pop culture image and adds text as an art product. When a GIF is shared, it is owned by the community that uses it. GIFs are meant to be shared. The strength of a GIF is how far it is shared and how easily it is recognized. They act as expressions of emotion, connection with a community, or spreading a message, but they are a collective experience for all.

Study Mentor Texts

Before making a GIF, we recommend studying mentor texts or GIFs you want to inspire student-creators to unveil the features of this genre. To do this, select several GIFs that would resonate with students, considering the age and readiness of your students. Ask what they notice about the various GIFs. Using an inquiry-based method, elicit the various features of a GIF. Some that might become apparent and that you will use in your assessment include the following:

1. Animation: GIFs can display a sequence of images or frames, creating the appearance of animation. This makes them ideal for short, looping animations.
2. Looping: One of the defining characteristics of GIFs is their ability to loop continuously. This means the animation will play over and over without stopping.
3. Text: Creative use of font in size, color, and type to create movement and communicate a message. Note: Not all GIFs have text; there may be sound or a sound bite.
4. Messaging: The animation, looping, text, and sound work together to communicate a message or commentary on a topic, which may be humorous, serious, or ironic (among other tones).

Steps for Content Creation

Before you start creating a GIF in Canva, ensure you have all your images, text, and media ready and saved on your computer. Additionally, identify the reason, audience, and goal for your GIF. This preparation will help you create a more focused and effective GIF. We like the GIF for school because GIF files can be directly embedded into documents, making them versatile for various uses and easy to submit to learning management systems (LMS). Ideally, you, the teacher, will model this process using an I do/We do method, but this will depend on the comfort of your student with the technology (Figure 5.6).

1. Open the Canva website and log in to your account.
2. Click on "Create a Design."
3. Select "Instagram Post (Square)" as your design format.

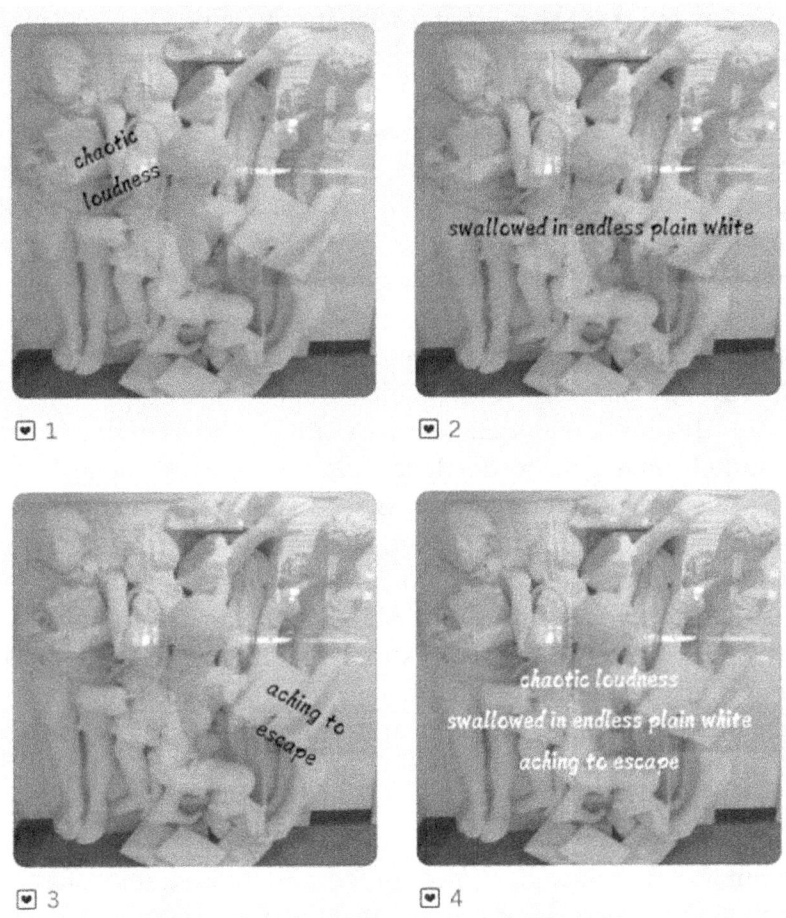

FIGURE 5.6 Steps to create and edit "Chaotic loudness" haiku GIF

4. Upload the images you want to use.
5. Drag and drop each image onto your design workspace, repeating the process for each image.
6. Use the "Text" tool to add text to your images.
7. Customize the text as needed, mixing up images and text to create variety.
8. Click on the "Share" button.
9. Select "Download."
10. Choose "File type: GIF" from the dropdown menu.
11. Click "Download" to save your GIF (automatically set to 20 seconds with five images).

By following these steps, you can create engaging GIFs in Canva and use them in various applications, including embedding them directly into documents.

We think that the animated social media design template is the best to start with (see Canva, n.d.). You can add images and adjust timing (it is present for 5 seconds, and see Figure 5.6 to see how you can edit several frames. You can adjust the length of each image. The last slide has a text effect of blurring. You might also try LICEcap to create a short GIF from the live movement of your screen (e.g., it records your short actions and repeats as GIFs do; see Chapter 9 for the GIF made with LICEcap).

In Chapter 3, we discussed the writing process in detail and included some ideas for feedback and revision. We suggest you schedule some class time for **peer feedback and revision**. After getting the GIF into a document, students can use the rubric to guide feedback that can inform revisions prior to publication. Also, as part of the writing workshop model, it will be important for you to show your own haiku GIF and model the process of giving genre-specific feedback, considering how this creation will live in the hallways of your school and the impact it will have on those that see the GIFs.

Publication

To publish the haiku GIF project for the school community, start by setting up a shared Google slide deck and have each student insert their GIF into a slide. Format the slides to be 8X8, but the standard slide works well, too. One tip is to number the slides in student order and have students put their names in the speaker notes. Once all the GIFs are added, send the slide deck to your internal broadcast engineer to incorporate the slides into the school's TV feed. Organize a silent gallery walk by sending students in groups to the various TVs throughout the school, allowing them to experience their GIFs displayed in the hallways in a new and engaging way. This display will not only be visible to students but also to school visitors during events such as sporting games and open houses. Finally, grade the project using the provided rubric and artist statement to evaluate each student's work (see Table A5.1 in Appendix for further processing and rubric; co-created with Jenn

FIGURE 5.7 Chaotic Loudness GIF QR Code

Yong Sanders). Here we see a revised GIF and artist statement for one learner's haiku GIF (Figure 5.7).

> I was surprised how crafting this made me stop and think more about the words I chose; for example, plain white is obvious, but the word "plain" adds an extension to my original meaning. I started by listing the obvious visuals I saw with this art piece and then thought about the meaning of their movements. In the GIF, I separated the lines into different images to show a movement that represented "escaping" and used colors to represent the haiku words. One peer suggested I pick a different word for "aching," but what I learned was that I felt that term sent more emotion and represented what I also felt when looking at this art.

Reflection

The complexity of a haiku, especially the significance of its third line, as explored in the genre study section, often goes unnoticed. This line typically introduces a shift or an "aha" moment, transforming the poem's narrative and providing a profound insight. Each student brings their unique perspective and creativity to this form, making the careful selection of words and the art of brevity crucial. When we encourage students to write haikus about their community and the people within it, we foster a sense of connection and humanize our schools. This practice allows students to see their surroundings through a poetic lens, transforming everyday experiences into moments of artistic reflection.

By turning our hallways into sources of inspiration and sharing haiku GIFs on hallway TV broadcasts, we offer students a platform to showcase their creativity and contribute to the school culture. Another way to share these is on a school Facebook feed or a device in a public school space. This project not only beautifies our physical spaces but also celebrates the diversity of thoughts and experiences within our community. The adaptability of this approach means it can be applied to various community spaces and topics, making it relevant across different content areas. Students are challenged to make thoughtful decisions about the poetic elements and the interplay of images and text in their GIFs, honing their skills in both literary and digital craftsmanship.

We encourage you to tailor these tools to fit your specific classroom and school needs, fostering a supportive environment where students can explore and express their ideas creatively. Crafting haiku GIFs requires practice and patience, and as students continue to create, their work will grow in sophistication and depth. Ultimately, the focus should be on the intentionality behind their choices and the insights gained through this artistic endeavor, celebrating both the journey and the finished product.

Reference List

Balaban, Y., & Çevik, İ. F. (2020). New forms of expression in the beginning of the internet; A research in the context of GIF and Doodle. *Turkish Studies-Information Technologies & Applied Sciences*, *15*(4), 417–430.

Canva. (n.d.). *Animated social media templates*. Canva. Retrieved August 18, 2024, from https://www.canva.com/animated-social-media/templates/

Dirk, K. (2010). Navigating genres. In C. Lowe & P. Zemliansky (Eds.), *Writing spaces: Readings on writing* (Vol. 1, pp. 249–262). WritingSpaces.org; Parlor Press; The WAC Clearinghouse. https://wac.colostate.edu/books/writingspaces/writingspaces1/

Eppink, J. (2014). A brief history of the GIF (so far). *Journal of Visual Culture*, *13*(3), 298–306.

Harris Baiocchi, R. (2004). *Urban Haiku*. Susaami Books.

Van Den Heuvel, C. (2000). *The Haiku anthology*. W. W. Norton & Company.

Voigts, E. (2018). Memes, GIFs, and remix culture: Compact appropriation in everyday digital life 1. In D. Cutchins, K. Krebs, & E. Voigts (Eds.), *The Routledge companion to adaptation* (pp. 390–402). Routledge.

Zhu, Q., & Wang, H. C. (2021). Is a GIF worth a thousand words? Understanding the use of dynamic graphical illustrations for procedural knowledge sharing on wikiHow. In *Proceedings of the 19th European Conference on Computer-Supported Cooperative Work: The International Venue on Practice-centred Computing on the Design of Cooperation Technologies*. European Society for Socially Embedded Technologies. https://doi.org/10.18420/ecscw2021_ep16

Appendix

TABLE A5.1 Rubric: Haiku GIF

Haiku GIF Rubric and Artist Statement	
Assignment Component	*Meet Expectations (2 pts)*
Final e-Poetry Submission	You submitted a complete, polished poetry artifact. In this final piece, you considered peer and facilitator feedback, and carefully edited the piece for form, style, grammar, language, technology, etc.
Poetry Craft Moves Standard: Write informative/explanatory texts to examine and convey complex ideas, concepts, and information clearly and accurately through the effective selection, organization, and analysis of content.	Informational Haiku • 3 lines • Meter 5-7-5 • Shift, or the turn to the third line, is reflective of an aha about the subject
Technology Component Standard: Use technology, including the Internet, to produce and publish writing and to interact and collaborate with others. https://iste.org/standards/students	GIF • Color(s) is symbolic or thematic • Symbolic objects (one or two) • Movement (animation of the image/text) that is meaningful or relevant to the shift (aha) in the poem with timing aligned • File .gif

(Continued)

TABLE A5.1 (*Continued*)

	Haiku GIF Rubric and Artist Statement
1 Revision Strategy	The final piece and/or artist statement demonstrates that at least one revision strategy from the course was attempted. (A writer may choose not to use a revision, but trying it out is an important part of the process.)
Artist Statement	Your artist statement discusses how X informed your written piece, identifies the craft moves and revision strategy you implemented, describes a significant aspect of your writing process or experience, and describes what you learned as a writer from this process.

Scoring Scale:

Meets Expectations (2 pts): Thoughtfully completed in a way that reflects course lessons and meets criteria.

Partially Developed (1): The product is only partially developed, or it reflects course lessons in a limited way. Revisit course activities and lessons or instructor feedback for further development.

Missing/Incomplete (0): The assignment is missing or incomplete to a degree that it is not able to be scored. Or the artifact does not reflect the assignment guidelines.

Artist Statement (handout offered during class)

- What surprised you about (topic) while you were crafting the project? Give a specific example. (For example... For instance...) What successes resulted from the project?
- Tell us about your process—how did you get from beginning to end in writing this piece?
- Which mentor texts had the biggest impact on your thinking and writing? (Name the author/colleague, name the text and explain how you used the mentor texts to inspire your writing.)
- Which craft elements and/or minilessons impacted the revision and meaning of your writing?
- Which peer feedback influenced your choices? Please cite classmates.
- What did you learn about the topic/context/subject of this piece that you may not have known or understood when you first began writing this?
- What do you understand about this mode and genre in particular that you may not have known or understood when you first began?
- What did you learn about yourself as a writer and content creator? (For example … For instance …)

6

Place-Based Poetry: Zip-Odes and YouTube Shorts

We are shaped by place. And place shapes us. Place-based writing is so much more than writing outdoors, though we recommend getting students outside the classroom with their notebooks or laptops as often as possible. In fact, place-based writing attends to the histories of a place and people's experiences of that place over time. Place-based writing is a culturally sustaining and proactive practice (Akkaya Yılmaz & Karakuş, 2018; Coughlin & Kirsch, 2010; Garcia & O'Donnell-Allen, 2015) because it centers the writers' cultures, identities, experiences, perspectives, people, and places. When we teach from this stance, we value local cultures and knowledges, and we consider the local and global systems that affect places and people. Indeed, our students are part of histories of place and experiences that inform their learning, lived experiences that we may not know about, so welcoming past and present places that shape our students is part of humanizing pedagogy.

In this unit of digital poetry, we want to draw on the critical pedagogy of place in particular, which prioritizes an understanding of connections among local and global contexts influenced by broader social, economic, and power systems (Azano, 2011). Critical pedagogy of place is a way of reading, writing, and creating texts that focus on the systems of power in a place. Our students' engagement with poetry and digital tools can surface and interrupt such power systems as they also leverage language and technology to shape place (see Figure 6.1 e-Poetry Framework for zip-ode shorts).

Plan with e-Poetry Framework

For this chapter, we will focus on a unit around genocide studies. Most states have some Holocaust education and/or genocide education studies unit at the middle and secondary levels. However, we think the activities shared here can be easily adapted for any summative assessment of student learning because the goal of this unit is for students to show what they learned about genocide (or any topic) by creating a series of digital shorts (under 60 seconds) with meaningful titles (100 characters) and descriptions (5000 characters). The purpose of the content is to inform the audience about what they learned using critical place theory or to show the relationship between social, economic, and power systems in the past and present. The purpose of literacy is to demonstrate critical media literacy in representing the place and people from history and today in ways that honor the memory of those who were killed while showing the present-day place and people, including implications of the past.

What Is the Learning Purpose?

The first decision for this assignment was to consider the standard and content, which is to inform their audience about what they learned using critical place theory or to show the relationship of social, economic, and power systems in the past and present. In this unit, the focus is on genocide, but this can also be any content. The purpose of literacy is to demonstrate critical media literacy in representing the place and people from history and today in ways that honor the memory of those who were killed while showing the present-day place and people, including implications of the past. We see this summative assessment as student-driven as our students use TikTok, Instagram, and YouTube as we write this chapter, drawing on the short digital video format.

Place-Based Poetry ◆ 97

e-Poetry Framework
ZIP-ODE SHORTS

Digital

Purpose & Choice
Student-driven. The students decided they wanted to show their learning in a series of shorts.

Mode & Choice
Informational-Argument Students will create digital shorts with facts about people & places they have studied from historic to contemporary.

Form & Choice
YouTube Short, 60 second video with a title and description using zip code poetry

Audience: Private to Public & Choice
The audience is the World Wide Web as the series of shorts will be shared on the student's social media platform of their choice. The students are over 15; if students are younger, this can be only the class.

Permanence & Choice
The student can choose faceless digital shorts and a non-identifiable account or with their face and on their social media account. The short can be deleted by the student.

Nature of Interaction & Choice
Shareable, interactive, set to remix or not depending on the creator's preference. Remixing will promote awareness, but may also lend itself to negative remixing.

Genre →

Donovan & Boutcher (2024)

FIGURE 6.1 e-Poetry Framework: Zip-ode Shorts

What Is the Mode?

Instead of a written composition or essay, we see the digital short as engaging our students in many decisions about what to **inform** their social media followers about genocide and how to be aware of the non-followers, possibly descendants of genocide or the diaspora of the region, who may come upon the videos and read the descriptions because of the keywords and hashtags associated with the post. This mode of communication is becoming the language currency of younger generations. The tone of the images, music, and text matters in humanizing the unimaginable atrocities and characterization of the culture.

What Is the Poetic Form?

In this chapter, we share the zip-ode poem with you. This is a way of attending to the geographic locations of various historical events along with the geographical location of the diaspora of the people impacted by the genocide in the past, including their descendants today, and the location of the student to show how place shapes people and how people can shape place. In the digital world, the concept of place is complicated further as the past and present, the physical and digital spaces of the creator and the audience intersect to continue to extend as the digital short is shared virally. With the use of tags and views, the algorithm pushes the content further into the meta space that has become a common digital "place" for all of us. The zip-ode poems the creator uses will have layers of meaning on the screen, while the creator-student will include more details in the description part of the digital post. In other words, the poetic form works with images, music, title, and description.

Who Is the Audience?

While the audience is always the teacher who is assessing learning, the audience of this unit is the followers of the student's social media, in addition to non-followers if the account is public and the algorithm pushes the content beyond the followers of the creator (see NEA, 2024, for further guidelines for social media in education). This is a setting that impacts the next feature of the e-Poetry Framework.

Who Will Interact with the Content? How?

The student's social media audience will be able to interact with the digital short by liking (thumbs up or heart) and/or commenting only if the creator allows that feature. Further, some platforms allow remixing of the content—the audio, the template of the video, the poem. Of course, the content on social media can always be screenshotted by the user, but the creator can also use a remix setting on YouTube, for example. The "insights" in Instagram, for example, or the "analytics" in YouTube, will show views and time spent watching the content (learn more about analytics here https://www.socialmediaexaminer.com/how-to-analyze-your-youtube-shorts/#:~:text=Navigate%20to%20the%20Content%20tab,any%20point%20on%20the%20graph). In other words, even if people do not like the video or comment, there is evidence of engagement otherwise, and the student knows that what they made is reaching an audience or informing an audience what the student learned.

How Permanent Is the Artifact?

The permanence of the shorts is different from other social media, such as Instagram stories. The "stories" have a limited amount of view time and then disappear from public view. The shorts (YouTube) or reels (Instagram) will live on the social media account as long as the creator wants it to be there, and the creator can decide if the content is public or private. For the sake of this project, the teacher will see the content, and then the student can technically delete it. Still, one idea of our e-poetry framework is illuminating how students can use social media to share what they are learning in school beyond the school classroom, to understand the reach of social media and the ethical considerations in creating a range of content—in this case, genocide education information. Another aspect of permanence is the extent to which the content is identifiable. Of course, the content is associated with an account, and to the degree the account has a student name and image (versus a handle or is a faceless account), the videos will be identifiable. Still, the student can choose to create faceless shorts, which means that the videos use images and video clips without the student's face shown. This is quite common on social media. A faceless social media campaign (i.e., via a digital short) is a strategy where the emphasis is placed on the message, movement, or cause rather than the individuals behind it. This approach can be powerful for various reasons:

1. **Focus on the Cause**: By not highlighting individuals, the campaign ensures that attention is centered on the message or issue at hand, reducing the risk of personal biases or distractions.
2. **Inclusivity and Unity**: It promotes a sense of collective action and community, as the campaign is presented as a unified effort rather than one led by specific individuals.
3. **Anonymity for Safety**: In some cases, maintaining anonymity can protect participants, especially if the campaign addresses controversial or sensitive issues that might provoke backlash.
4. **Viral Potential**: Faceless campaigns can often go viral more easily as they encourage widespread participation without the need for personal recognition or credit.
5. **Broad Appeal**: Without focusing on individuals, the campaign can appeal to a broader audience, making it easier for diverse groups to connect with the cause.

Learn the Poem Form

Invented in 2015, the zip-ode is a five-line poem about where you live, written in the form of your zip code. Write the numbers of your zip code down the left-hand side of the page. Each number determines the number of words in that line. If you have a zero in your zip code, that line is a wild card. You can leave it blank, insert an emoji or symbol, or use any number of words between 1 and 9.

We learned about this form from Illinois educator, Mo Daley, who participated in The Poetry Foundation's Summer Poetry Teachers Institute in Miami. The zip-ode, an original form invented by O, Miami (n.d.; a community-based organization for amplifying Miami's people), is designed to transform your zip code into an occasion for place-based, lyrical celebration. The form has been featured in media outlets such as *The Takeaway* and *The Washington Post*. For places without a zip code, Kris Archie came up with a solution for areas that have postal codes (a combination of letters and numbers) instead of zip codes. When the line has a letter instead of a number, that line has one word that must begin with that letter.

Here is Sarah's poem about Stillwater, Oklahoma, and the college town:

Stillwater

7 Non-carbonated or no current visible here.
4 This stream of college
0 生
7 flows in football & frats and RV lots
5 stills in holidays 'n' hot summers

Sarah used the metaphor of water throughout this zip-ode poem, even though Oklahoma is quite dry. The water represents the students who flow in and out of this college town. Sarah is shaped by this place as a new resident, having grown up and lived in Chicago most of her life, so she brings an outsider perspective to this poem.

As we think about this form, we want to consider the potential as an ode or celebration of place, but also, in light of our students' lives and the topic of genocide for this unit, the potential concerns when surfacing memories and details of a place or zip code area. For example, much of Oklahoma is Indigenous land. The zip-ode poem could reflect that the area of Stillwater, Oklahoma, was home to several indigenous peoples, including the Osage, Ponca, Kiowa, Pawnee, Lenape, Kiikaapoi (Kickapoo), and Wichita. The Lenape tribe and their ancestors lived in Stillwater Township for 12,000 years before European contact. For Osage, Ponca, Kiowa, and Pawnee, these tribes called the creek "Still Water" because of its calm currents. There are also legends that cattlemen found water there during dry years and that David Payne, a leader of the Boomers, named the town after the creek.

Celebrating a place without acknowledging its complexities can come off as superficial or dismissive of serious issues. Encourage students to explore and reflect on both the positive and challenging aspects of their community. Create a balanced narrative that respects the full history and experiences of the place.

Study Mentor Texts

As you begin working with zip-odes, you can first support students in crafting personal zip-odes. Students may have personal experiences with the place that could be painful or triggering. Create a safe and supportive environment where students feel comfortable sharing their thoughts and experiences. Showing a range of poem mentors is important so that students can see they can write poetry and write about a place from a variety of angles.

We like beginning with a study of mentor texts as an inquiry-based method of surfacing the guidelines of a form and where poets choose to modify or make the form their own. You can start by showing Sarah's poem, or you can start with "Lost" by Stacey L. Joy (2024). In Stacey's poem, you can see her adding numbers and letters to the left of the numbers. This is a clever adaptation of the poem to turn it into a narrative or short story that leaves the reader wondering what happened.

Lost by Stacey L. Joy (2024)

19 sixty eight
m0ved in, family
 0f
 f0ur
w8 until 2010 to lose it all

And this poem by Donnetta Norris is another great mentor text to show students a way of thinking about the audience. In this poem, Donnetta is talking directly to the reader, using the poem to answer the question: Where is Mansfield, TX? She also chose to leave the 0 line empty. You might ask the students, "how many have a zero in their zip code?" and "what options do they have for that?"

Where is Mansfield? by Donnetta Norris (2024)

7 Mansfield, TX! Where is that? Oh, about
6 30 minutes south of Dallas. Do
0
6 you know where the Cowboys play?
3 We're near there.

Finally, we like to look at three mentor texts so that students have a range to inspire their writing. Let's see how one poet used emojis. This next poem is from Cheri Mann, who wanted to express what is not in her small town. This can be read as celebratory or derogatory, but the reader has to look closely at the emojis, we think, to gauge the tone.

40050 by Cheri Mann (2024)

4 Not really much here
0 🫠
0 😌
5 Not even a single stoplight
0.

After looking at a few mentor texts, you are ready to model your own zip-ode poem in front of your students. We recommend not skipping this step so that you can model and do a little think-aloud about how the zip-odes could inadvertently reinforce stereotypes or negative judgments. As you study the mentor texts and write your zip-ode, foster discussions about empathy, diversity, and respect.

The poem could also lead to polarized views or debates among students, particularly if their experiences of the place differ significantly. Facilitate constructive dialogue and ensure that discussions remain respectful and inclusive. Teach students how to listen actively and respond thoughtfully to different viewpoints.

At this point, you can stop here to study and write about zip-odes. This lesson can be adapted to characters in novels, important places in a unit of study, and historical or current events. However, we are extending the zip-ode work to promote global awareness and meet some content area requirements around genocide education.

Content Background

You are the content area expert and have learned alongside your students as they studied a novel, researched a literary period, and made inquiries into a time and place. For this chapter, we are focusing on genocide education.

Just a note here that we will emphasize throughout: Genocide education scholars firmly advise against showing any deceased humans in photographs on social media or the classroom. Further, we add a few other pedagogical guidelines to teaching about the Holocaust and genocide, in case you have not received training in teaching about atrocities. Teaching teenagers about the Holocaust and genocide is a sensitive and challenging task that requires careful consideration and respect. See Table 6.1.

Incorporating these tips can help create a respectful and impactful learning environment that honors the memory of the victims and fosters a deep, empathetic understanding of these tragic events.

In Sarah's junior high English language arts class, she taught a 2-day unit around the Armenian Genocides using a resource from The Genocide Education Project (n.d.) website (see References for full PDF to this unit).

Briefly, The Armenian Genocide was a systematic mass murder and expulsion of ethnic Armenians carried out by the Ottoman Empire during World War I. The genocide is generally considered to have started on April 24, 1915, when the Ottoman authorities rounded up, arrested, and later executed several hundred Armenian intellectuals and community leaders in Constantinople (modern-day Istanbul).

The roots of the genocide lie in the declining fortunes of the Ottoman Empire and rising ethnic tensions. Armenians, a Christian minority, were often viewed with concern by the Muslim-majority

TABLE 6.1 Holocaust Education Guidance

Five tips scholars of genocide studies often emphasize on what not to do (Auron & Ruzga, 2005; Avraham, 2013; Marks, 2017; Totten, 2004; United States Holocaust Memorial Museum, 2016):

1. **Avoid Graphic Imagery and Sensationalism**
   - Why: Graphic images or sensationalized accounts can be traumatizing and may lead to desensitization or disengagement.
   - What to do instead: Use age-appropriate materials that convey the gravity of the events without overwhelming students. Focus on personal stories and testimonies to humanize history.

2. **Don't Simplify or Generalize:**
   - Why: Simplifying complex historical events can lead to misunderstandings and diminish the significance of the genocide.
   - What to do instead: Provide context and detail to help students understand the historical, political, and social complexities. Encourage critical thinking and analysis.

3. **Avoid Comparisons that Rank or Measure Suffering:**
   - Why: Comparing the genocides to different events can be disrespectful and minimize the unique suffering experienced by victims.
   - What to do instead: Treat each genocide as a distinct event with its own specific causes, processes, and consequences. Respect the unique historical and cultural contexts. There's value in comparing the characteristics, stages, effects, etc., so that students can see that genocides have similarities and differences, allowing them to better identify genocide.

4. **Don't Use Role-Playing Exercises:**
   - Why: Role-playing can trivialize the experiences of victims and survivors, and it can cause emotional distress among students.
   - What to do instead: Use primary sources, survivor testimonies, and reflective discussions to engage students empathetically and thoughtfully.

5. **Avoid Presenting the Genocide as an Inevitable Event:**
   - Why: Portraying the genocide as inevitable can lead to fatalism and a lack of understanding about human agency and the importance of resistance and resilience.
   - What to do instead: Emphasize the choices and actions of individuals and groups, both perpetrators and rescuers, to highlight the impact of human decisions and the possibility of moral courage.

Ottoman rulers, especially during a time of increasing Armenian activism and calls for reform.

Over the next several years, the Ottoman government orchestrated a series of brutal campaigns against the Armenian population. The genocide was characterized by mass deportations, forced marches, and massacres. Armenians were systematically removed from their homes and sent on death marches to the Syrian desert. Along the way, they were subjected to mass shootings, starvation, dehydration, and other atrocities. Women and children were often abducted, raped, or sold into slavery. Many children were sent to orphanages for Turkification, meaning their hair was cut, and they were not permitted to speak Armenian or practice Christianity. Many were raised without even knowing they were once Armenian (Gzoyan et al., 2019; Gzoyan & Galustyan, 2021).

Estimates of the number of Armenians killed during the genocide vary, but it is widely accepted that between 1 and 1.5 million Armenians perished. Virtually all Armenian personal properties and community institutions (schools, hospitals, churches, community centers, etc.) were destroyed or stolen and transferred to Turks.

The aftermath of the genocide saw a significant Armenian diaspora as survivors fled to various parts of the world, including the Middle East, Europe, and the Americas. The Turkish government, successor to the Ottoman Empire, has consistently denied that the events constituted a genocide, arguing instead that the deaths were a result of inter-ethnic conflict, disease, and famine during the tumultuous war years.

The Armenian Genocide has been recognized by many countries and international organizations. The blue spruce trees planted at the Armenian Genocide Museum-Institute are symbolic of such recognition. Ongoing research at the institute is archiving artifacts and oral histories as evidence. Still, efforts continue to seek global recognition and justice for the atrocities committed. Specifically, Turkey refuses to recognize it and supports Azerbaijan's ethnic cleansing and forced exodus of the indigenous Armenian population of the former Soviet "autonomous region" of Nagorno Karabagh (Artsakh) in 2023. Armenian people continue to speak Armenian, teach the language, and practice Christianity. They are reclaiming their heritage. The Tufenkian Foundation's mission—Rebuild. Restore. Revive.—is a motto many Armenians follow (n.d.). Efforts include reforestation and cultural restoration. Matenadaran (n.d.), a museum of manuscripts, houses approximately 20,000 manuscripts in Armenian and other languages. As a research institute, they restore and study manuscripts dating back to the 5th century, some still being recovered from the diaspora who survived the 1915 genocide.

On the first day, students learn a brief history of the Armenian Genocide and read *IWitness* personal accounts (see full link in References). Sarah reads a 1939 quote by Hitler on display at the United States Holocaust Memorial Museum (n.d.), leading to a discussion about the possibility that the Holocaust may have played out differently had the genocide against the Armenians been acknowledged, the perpetrators held accountable, and reparations have been made.

On the second day, students read a personal account by Henry Morgenthau, the American Ambassador to the Ottoman Empire, about the documents and telegrams that show evidence of the Armenian Genocide (see Gibson report, 2017). Students then reflect on what they know and what to know. Next, we read portions of *The Convention on the Prevention and Punishment of the Crime of Genocide (the United Nations' Definition of Genocide* [1948]). Together, we define "genocide" and raise the point that many scholars have a much narrower definition. We consider previous genocides (Native Americans) and human rights abuses and ask students to explore patterns that emerge. Students take notes that they use for their facts and further inquiry. We conclude with a Pledge Against Genocide. This pledge was created by Genocide Watch and is then returned to the organization as students also sign up for alerts on their Instagram and through email.

What other places are important to Armenian people to show their resilience and that they are still here? The main idea of this unit is *to recognize* and show the place, existence, and growth of the Armenian people. When Sarah visited Armenia, several young people said they didn't want to be known as victims or a minority. They have been living in this region for centuries and have kept their ancient language and culture alive.

Zip-ode poems around Armenia surface global understanding for students because zip and postal codes do not look the same across the world. Here are some of the important people and places in the very short unit that we studied. Looking at what we know about these people and places, we develop zip-ode poems to use in our digital shorts (see Table 6.2).

TABLE 6.2 Developing Content for Zip-ode Shorts

Resource	Notes for the Zip-ode Short
IWitness (n.d.)	• Alice Shipley, born 1904, Diyarbakır (Diyarbakır, Turkey) • Aurora Mardiganian, born 1901, Çemişgezek (Tunceli, Turkey) • There are many others.
Short Essays for Young Adults from *Just YA*	• "On Being Armenian" by Aida Zilelian (2024a) • "Zilelian from Zile" by Aida Zilelian (2024b) • "Compulsory Service" by S. (Anonymous, 2024)
Henry Morgenthau	• American Ambassador to the Ottoman Empire • Address: The U.S. Embassy in Turkey today: U.S. Consulate Istanbul, İstinye, Poligon Cd. No:75, 34460 Sarıyer/İstanbul, Türkiye
United Holocaust Memorial Museum	• Named the Armenian Genocide in 1939 (before The Genocide Convention) • Address: United States Holocaust Memorial Museum, 100 Raoul Wallenberg Pl SW, Washington, DC 20024
Armenian Genocide Museum-Institute (n.d.)	• Memorial Description and History (see References) • Blue Spruce trees (Mikayelyan & Papazyan, (2021)) • Address: 8, Tsitsernakaberd Armenian Genocide Memorial Complex, 8 Tsitsernakaberd Hwy, Yerevan 0028, Armenia
United Nations	• The Genocide Convention (Lemkin, 1945) • Address: 760 United Nations Plaza, Manhattan, New York City, New York, US
Tufenkian Foundation	• After the 2020 Artsakh War, a conflict involving Azerbaijan and Armenia over the region, the foundation focused on infrastructure, education, economic development, the housing of wounded soldiers, and livelihood opportunities. • During the blockade and ethnic cleansing of Artsakh, they provided food relief, evacuation, and shelter support. • After the ethnic cleansing of September 2023, they focused on resettlement projects for displaced compatriots from Artsakh to help them establish a dignified life in Armenia. • Address: Tufenkian Historic Yerevan Hotel, 48 Hanrapetutyan St, Yerevan 0010, Armenia

(*Continued*)

TABLE 6.2 *(Continued)*

Resource	Notes for the Zip-ode Short
Matenadaran (n.d.)	• Matenadaran was registered in UNESCO's "World Memory" list in 1997 and is considered one of the most important places for the preservation and development of Armenian national memory. • Matenadaran is a prominent institution in Armenia that houses the intellectual heritage of its people. • Address: 53 Mesrop Mashtots Ave, Yerevan 0009, Armenia
The Armenian Rug Society "Adopt-a-Loom Initiative" with Silk Road Hotel	• The Foundation has been teaching free rug weaving and embroidery classes to more than 100 children and adults alike at its headquarters at the Silk Road Hotel. • The Society emphasizes how important it is to encourage others to learn the ancient Armenian craft of weaving as an integral part of helping to revive this Armenian national craft that once was a ubiquitous tradition in so many households across historic Armenia. • Address: 53, 2 Aygedzor St, Yerevan 0019, Armenia

Learn the Tech: YouTube Short

What we call a digital short or a short video in this chapter has variations across several social media platforms. TikTok, which launched globally in September 2016, quickly became a dominant platform for short-form video content, allowing users to create 15- to 60-second videos with a wide array of effects, music, and editing tools. Facebook Stories in 2017 and Instagram Reels (both under Meta), launched on August 5, 2020, were developed to compete directly with TikTok, which had gained significant popularity, especially among younger users. Reels allow users to create short, engaging videos up to 60 seconds long, equipped with various editing tools such as audio, effects, and creative enhancements. This feature was introduced to increase user engagement, extend the time users spend on the platform, and provide new opportunities for content creators and brands to interact with their audience and generate revenue through advertising.

Recognizing TikTok's success and the growing demand for such content, YouTube introduced Shorts in September 2020 (initially in beta in India) and globally in March 2021. YouTube Shorts enables users to create and share 15 to 60-second videos with similar editing tools, aiming to adapt to the shifting preferences of users, particularly the younger demographic. This addition sought to diversify YouTube's content offerings and provide new monetization avenues for creators, thereby attracting a broader range of content creators to the platform.

Students can create the zip-ode poem using the video tool on any of these platforms. There are many features within each app, so the student, as the content creator, has to make many decisions related to length, as evident in the "short," but also in image, sound, and text (see Table 6.3 Digital short decision-making).

It is up to the teacher and school to decide to what extent they want students to use their phones to create the short. As of 2024, several states have implemented bans on TikTok, primarily on government devices and wi-fi networks, due to concerns about security. While writing this chapter, most teachers have access to a free educator account on Canva.com, and/or schools have an account that students can use on their school-issued technology devices. For this reason, we will recommend using Canva, for now, during class time and then asking students to post their shorts to their preferred social media accounts as an option.

Study Mentor Texts

As with the zip-ode and other digital poetry we discuss in this book, we recommend beginning with a study of mentor texts to ground the learning in inquiry. While one option is to tell the students what is required in a digital short, we prefer eliciting the criteria from what students already know and notice in several mentor texts.

Gather several examples of YouTube Shorts that are appropriate and relevant to your students' lives to study what makes them effective (remember, we already reviewed poetry mentor

TABLE 6.3 Digital Short Decision-Making Table

Category	Sub-Category	Details and Decisions
Size		1080x1920 px
Length		Automatically, 5 seconds on Canva
		60-second max on YouTube, but set their creator at 15 seconds
		90 seconds max on Instagram Reel
Publishing		Same day
		Schedule the date and time: YouTube between 12–3 p.m. and 7–10 p.m.; Instagram, Monday through Thursday between 9 a.m. and 12 p.m. PST
Image	Picture	Original or stock; Quality and relevance to the topic
	Video	Self-shot or faceless; Length (15–60 seconds); Quality and editing style
	Style	Animated or live-action; Filters and effects to use
	Thumbnail	Custom-made or auto-generated; Text overlays; Visual appeal and relevance
Sound	Speech	Original recording or voice-over; Clarity and tone; Scripted or impromptu
	Music	Background music choice (genre, mood); Volume balance with speech; Royalty-free or licensed music
	Effects	Sound effects (e.g., transitions, emphasis); Volume levels; Timing and relevance to the content
Text	Title	Attention-grabbing; Keywords for search engine optimization (SEO); Length and clarity
	Description	Brief summary; Keywords and hashtags; Links and call-to-action
	Hashtags	Begin with a #, written within a post or comment to highlight it and facilitate a search for it
	On-screen Text	Captions for accessibility; Emphasis on key points; Font style and size
Engagement	Call-to-Action	Prompts to like, comment, subscribe; Interactive questions or challenges; Clear and concise
Audience	Target Audience	Age group; Interests and preferences; Cultural relevance
Branding	Consistency	Alignment with personal or channel brand; Use of logo or signature style; Consistent tone and voice
Analytics	Performance	Monitoring views, likes, and comments; Analyzing audience retention; Adjusting future content based on data

texts earlier in this chapter). Invite students to notice the relationship between the sound, texts, image, title, hashtags, and description. Illuminate and discuss the range of choices the creator had to make. Ask students to discuss and evaluate which ones are "good" or "effective" and which creators are making decisions they'd like to try in their short creations. After you elicit these creator moves, you can show them Table 6.3, Digital Short Decision-Making Table. The table can be a reference for decision-making.

To gather some mentor texts, we asked students to share some of their favorite YouTubers. Sarah spent some time sifting through the suggestions to find some that show a range of creator moves. It is important to select examples that feature place and how that place shapes the meaning of the video or impacts the creator.

Sarah narrowed down the mentor texts we'd study to Joe Martin and Taylor Swift. Joe Martin is a 25-year-old solo traveler from the UK who is vlogging around the world. Show the short video about his trip to Pakistan and ask students what they notice (Martin, 2024). There are a series of short video clips within the digital short. He is using voice-over narration and captions. The title is descriptive: "Why aren't more people visiting here?" and the title also has an emoji and three hashtags: #pakistan, #travel, #pakistani. Joe shows himself in the video engaging with the place and explaining each shot for its beauty and what he learned from his guides.

Depending on your students and their interests, you might look at Taylor Swift's YouTube Short (see Swift, 2024). In this short, there is a series of clips walking through doors and hallways of a mock department office of a school, it seems. The creator moves toward a bulletin board that includes details about "The Tortured Poets" release day. There is only the sound of a ticking clock (or typewriter) and a door squeaking—no captions, no voice-over. The title is "The TTPD Timetable" without hashtags or a description. This video shows how to build toward the moment, and we see how the zip-ode poem could be the concluding shot of the video (see Figure 6.2 for a QR code to access a template).

FIGURE 6.2 Canva example QR code.

Poem and Tech with Content

For content, you can divide up various topics around the area of focus. For this unit, we invited students to select a place we studied and then research facts about that place. Each student had a unique combination of the place and detail or angle they wanted to take. For example, the Tufenkian Historic Yerevan Hotel is one place, but students could choose to focus on 1) the symbolism of the carpets, 2) any of the Tufenkian Foundation's initiatives, 3) travel or tourism to promote a vibrant image of Yerevan, Armenia, and/or 4) the youth worker gives tours and presentations.

Sarah selected the Tufenkian Foundation and crafted a poem using the zip code of the Tufenkian Historic Yerevan Hotel to celebrate symbols of Armenian carpets and how they show the resilience of the Armenian people. Sarah borrowed from Cheri Mann's poem (2024), using emojis:

    0 🐢 protection and support
    0 🦉 wisdom, strength, courage
    1 Armenia
    0 ∞ *we have always been here*

After creating the poem, Sarah wrote a description of the poem to include with the digital short:

> Explore the intricate beauty and profound symbolism of Armenian carpets at the Tufenkian Hotel in Yerevan. Join us on a journey through the gallery where the dragon symbolizes protection and support, the tree of life embodies wisdom, strength, and courage, and the symbol of eternity reflects the enduring presence and resilience of the Armenian people. Learn about the rich history and cultural heritage of these stunning carpets, and how they continue to nurture and celebrate this ancient land. Don't miss the chance to delve into this fascinating art form through our guided tours and detailed information sessions. Subscribe for more insights into Armenian culture and heritage!

This description borrows from the Joe Martin mentor text with a celebratory feel and an invitation to visit and explore. The next step is to create the digital short.

Using Canva and focusing on YouTube Shorts for this section, we will walk you through the process of creating a Zipode Short. Creating a YouTube Short using Canva involves a series of straightforward steps, ensuring that your video content is engaging and optimized for the platform's short-form video format. See the QR code for Sarah's Canva example (Figure 6.2). See Figure 6.3 for the screenshot of the digital short.

1. **Start by Visiting the Canva Website or Opening the App.** You'll need to sign up if you don't have an account. If you already have an account, simply log in. Canva offers a user-friendly interface with a range of templates, making it easy for both beginners and seasoned creators to design content.
2. **Select the Right Format.** Once logged in, click on the "Create a design" button. In the search bar, type "YouTube Shorts" to find the specific template designed for vertical

Place-Based Poetry ♦ 115

video. Canva's template library is tailored to fit the 9:16 aspect ratio required for YouTube Shorts, ensuring your video is perfectly formatted for the platform.

3. **Choose a Template or Start from Scratch**. Sarah started from scratch for your zip-ode example featuring the Armenian carpets at the Tufenkian Historic Yerevan Hotel. Canva offers a variety of pre-designed templates suitable for YouTube Shorts. Students can browse through the options and select one that fits the tone of

FIGURE 6.3 Tufenkian Zip-ode Short screenshot. Image by author.

their message—if it is somber related to genocide harm or more joyful related to Armenian culture and resilience, for example. Students can use the features within Canva or download Creative Commons images and music to customize the background, add text, and incorporate elements like images, icons, or illustrations to enhance your video's visual appeal. Again, these would need to be relevant to the zip-ode. Students can explain their decision-making—as this is about choices and not about perfection—in the Artist Statement that accompanies their video and rubric. See Appendix at the end of this chapter.

4. **Add and Edit Your Content.** Use Canva's drag-and-drop editor to add text, images, videos, and other media. For YouTube Shorts, keep your content concise and engaging. Add text overlays, animations, and transitions to make your video dynamic. Canva's library includes a wide range of fonts, colors, and graphics, allowing you to align the design with your brand or theme. See Figure 6.4 for how to add text such as descriptions and hashtags.

5. **Incorporate Music and Voice Overs**: To make your YouTube Short more engaging, add background music

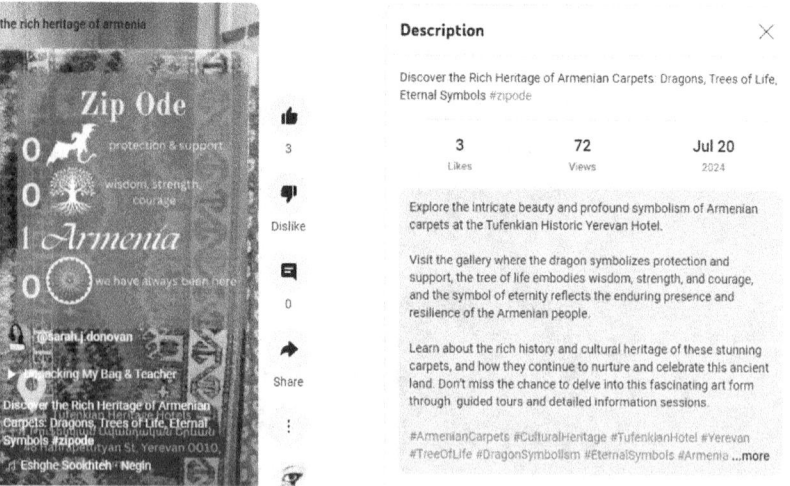

FIGURE 6.4 Sarah's Tufenkian Zip-ode Short published on YouTube (see Donovan, 2024)

or a voice-over. Canva provides a collection of royalty-free music tracks that you can browse and add to your video. Adjust the volume and timing to ensure the music complements your visuals without overpowering them.

After making a draft of the digital short, use the **peer review protocol** from Chapter 4 and the decision-making table (see Table 4.2 or 4.3), to prepare for publishing. During this step, students will preview the digital shorts to check for any adjustments needed. They can make sure the text is legible, the timing of transitions is smooth, and the overall flow is engaging. Canva's preview feature allows you to see how your video will look once published, helping you make necessary tweaks. This is a great opportunity for peers to discuss the tone and information conveyed in the digital short to be sure it honors the place and shows how the place has been shaped by history or the present. The students can discuss whether or not it is meaningful to have their own voice and image in the video to show the impact of the learning on them as someone who now understands the place, people, and history better.

Publication

Students can download their Canva video or leave it on the platform for you to assess and view one another's video and comment. You can also have students download the video from Canva and upload it to Google Classroom (or another learning management system) as their publication. From there, you might combine them all into a longer video (on YouTube or consider Adobe for education). You can decide who sees the video and how students engage with it. Because likes and comments are so important with social media as a sign of engagement, we encourage you to allow class time for students to view and comment on one another's work. Use the commenting guide in Chapter 4 (ISTE, 2024) to support students in naming the specific features of the poem and technology in their comments.

If you decide to publish the Zip-ode Shorts onto YouTube, you can have students move to the YouTube platform. Select the video file from your computer and fill in the details, such as title, description, and tags. Ensure you use relevant keywords and hashtags to increase the visibility of your short (see Table A6.1 in Appendix for further processing and rubric).

Reflection

Using poetry and technology to explore the concept of place allows students to delve into the ways in which environments shape us and how we, in turn, influence these spaces. Through the creation of zip-ode poems, teachers can guide students in reflecting on their personal experiences and connections to various places, both past and present. This poetic form enables learners to articulate their feelings and observations about their surroundings, fostering a deeper understanding and appreciation of the places that impact their lives. By transitioning from writing these poems to developing digital shorts that explore new places, students can continuously expand their perspectives and develop a richer sense of place.

The digital short, particularly in the form of YouTube videos, provides an excellent medium for students to express their understanding of place. This format encourages the integration of sound, image, text, hashtags, and descriptions to shape the tone and convey the message about a particular location through multimodalities. Creating these videos not only enhances students' technical skills but also helps them critically analyze how different elements contribute to the overall portrayal of place. This approach fosters creativity and allows students to engage with their audience on a deeper level, making their exploration of place more dynamic and impactful.

While this chapter has centered on the Armenian Genocide, the strategies discussed can be applied to a wide range of topics and locations. The rubric provided throughout the book serves as a valuable tool to guide the craft of content creation, emphasizing decision-making and intention over mere aesthetic appeal. We also encourage students to write an artist statement to illuminate and offer a rationale for their choices. Crafting these digital shorts takes time and practice; the more students create, the more sophisticated their work will become. Ultimately, the goal is to develop thoughtful and intentional content that resonates with audiences and reflects the profound impact of place on our lives.

Reference List

Akkaya Yılmaz, M., & Karakuş, U. (2018). The impact of place based education approach on student achievement in social studies. *Review of International Geographical Education Online (RIGEO)*, *8*(3), 500–516.

Anonymous. (2024). *Compulsory service. Just YA*. Open OkState: Ethical ELA.

Auron, Y., & Ruzga, R. (2005). *The pain of knowledge: Holocaust and genocide issues in education*. Transaction.

Avraham, D. (2013). The problem with using historical parallels as a method in Holocaust and genocide teaching. *Intercultural Education*, *21*(S1), 33–40. https://doi.org/10.1080/14675986.2013.815832

Azano, A. (2011). The possibility of place: One teacher's use of place-based instruction for English students in a rural high school. *Journal of Research in Rural Education*, *26*, 1–33.

Coughlin, C. A., & Kirch, S. A. (2010). Place-based education: A transformative activist stance. *Cultural Studies of Science Education*, *5*(4), 911–921. https://doi.org/10.1007/s11422-010-9290-6

Donovan, S. J. [@sarah.j.donovan]. (2024, July 20). *Discover the rich heritage of Armenian carpets: Dragons, trees of life, eternal symbols #zipode* [Video]. YouTube. https://www.youtube.com/watch?v=G2TZE8arBbg

Garcia, A., & O'Donnell-Allen, C. (2015). *Pose, wobble, flow: A culturally proactive approach to literacy instruction*. Teachers College Press.

Genocide Education Project. (n.d.). *Two-day lesson plan: Introduction to genocide.* https://genocideeducation.org/wp-content/uploads/2017/04/GenEd-Two-Day-Lesson.pdf

Genocide Museum-Institute. (n.d.). *Description and history*. Retrieved August 18, 2024, from http://www.genocide-museum.am/eng/Description_and_history.php

Gibson, C. (2017, April 24). *Recently discovered telegram reveals evidence for Armenian genocide*. NPR. https://www.npr.org/2017/04/24/525441639/recently-discovered-telegram-reveals-evidence-for-armenian-genocide

Gzoyan, E., Galustyan, R., & Khachatryan, S. (2019). Reclaiming children after the Armenian genocide: Neutral house in Istanbul. *Holocaust and Genocide Studies, 33*(3), 395–411.

Gzoyan, E., & Galustyan, R. (2021). Forced marriages as a tool of genocide: The Armenian case. *The International Journal of Human Rights, 25*(10), 1724–1743.

International Society for Technology in Education. (2024). *ISTE educator standards*. ISTE. https://iste.org/standards/educators

IWitness. (n.d.). *IWitness - Education through genocide testimony*. https://iwitness.usc.edu/home

Joy, S. (2024). Lost. *Ethical ELA*. https://www.ethicalela.com/zip-code-poem/

Lemkin, R. (1945). Genocide - a modern crime. *Free World, 9*, 39.

Mann, C. (2024). 40050 *Ethical ELA*. https://www.ethicalela.com/zip-code-poem/

Marks, M. J. (2017). Teaching the Holocaust as a cautionary tale. *Social Studies, 108*(4), 129–135. https://doi.org/10.1080/00377996.2017.1340781

Martin, J. [@joemartintravel]. (2024, August 18). *Why aren't more people visiting here?* [Video]. YouTube. https://youtube.com/shorts/O7Q_VpAb8u4

Matenadaran. (n.d.). *Matenadaran: The Mesrop Mashtots Institute of Ancient Manuscripts*. Retrieved August 18, 2024, from https://matenadaran.am/en/matenadaran/home/

Mikayelyan, S., & Papazyan, T. (2021). *Armenian genocide: Historical and cultural aspects* (Vol. 6, No. 2, pp. 74–89). International Journal of Armenian Genocide Studies. Retrieved August 18, 2024, from https://agmipublications.asnet.am/wp-content/uploads/2022/02/ijags2021_vol.6_n.2_74-89.pdf

NEA. (2024). Social media in education. National Educator Association: *NEA Advice Blog*. https://www.nea.org/social-media 1 February 2024

Norris, D. (2024). Where is Mansfield? *Ethical ELA*. https://www.ethicalela.com/zip-code-poem/

O, Miami. (n.d.). *O, Miami Poetry Festival*. Retrieved August 18, 2024, from https://omiami.org/

Swift, T. [@TaylorSwift]. (2024, April 16). *The TTPD timetable* [Video]. YouTube. https://www.youtube.com/shorts/RlDSGLHcZy0

Totten, S. (2004). *Teaching about genocide: Issues, approaches, and resources*. Information Age Publishing.

Tufenkian Foundation. (n.d.). *Tufenkian Foundation*. Retrieved August 18, 2024, from https://www.tufenkian.org/

United States Holocaust Memorial Museum. (n.d.). *Exhibit on Hitler's reference to Armenians (1939)*. Washington, DC.

United States Holocaust Memorial Museum. (2016). *Teaching about genocide.* https://www.ushmm.org/educators/teaching-about-the-holocaust/teaching-about-genocide

United Nations. (1948). *Convention on the prevention and punishment of the crime of genocide.* https://www.un.org/en/genocideprevention/documents/atrocity-crimes/Doc.1_Convention%20on%20the%20Prevention%20and%20Punishment%20of%20the%20Crime%20of%20Genocide.pdf

Yılmaz, M. A., & Karakuş, U. (2018). The impact of place based education approach on student achievement in social studies. *Review of International Geographical Education Online*, *8*(3), 500–516.

Zilelian, A. (2024a). On being Armenian. *Just YA*. Open OkState: EthicalELA.

Zilelian, A. (2024b). Zilelian from Zile. *Just YA*. Open Okstate: EthicalELA.

Appendix

TABLE A6.1 Rubric: Zip-ode Short Rubric and Artist Statement

	Zip-Ode Short Rubric and Artist Statement
Assignment Component	*Meet Expectations (2 pts)*
Final e-Poetry Submission	You submitted a complete, polished poetry artifact. In this final piece, you considered peer and facilitator feedback and carefully edited the piece for form, style, grammar, language, technology, etc.

(Continued)

TABLE A6.1 (*Continued*)

	Zip-Ode Short Rubric and Artist Statement
Assignment Component	*Meet Expectations (2 pts)*
Poetry Craft Moves Standard: Write informative/explanatory texts to examine and convey complex ideas, concepts, and information clearly and accurately through the effective selection, organization, and analysis of content. Standard: Write arguments to support claims in an analysis of substantive topics or texts using valid reasoning and relevant and sufficient evidence.	Informational-Argumentative Zip-Ode • Lines follow the zip or postal code of the place • Number of words or symbols relate to the number in the zip or postal code • Content draws on research and course content • Tone is respectful and relevant to the topic to teach the audience about the past and present of this place, including its significance
Technology Component Standard: Use technology, including the Internet, to produce and publish writing and to interact and collaborate with others. https://iste.org/standards/students	Digital Short • Image is a photo or video relevant to the content of the poem • Sound can be music, voice-over, or sound effects relevant to the place • Text overlays include the poem and or additional information; font and style are visible and meaningful to the tone and content • Title, description, and hashtags contain additional information with an argument/persuasion, encouraging the audience to learn more • File .mp4
1 Revision Strategy	The final piece and/or artist statement demonstrates that at least one revision strategy from the course was attempted. (A writer may choose not to use a revision but trying it out is an important part of the process.)
Artist Statement	Your artist statement discusses how X informed your written piece, identifies the craft moves and revision strategy you implemented, describes a significant aspect of your writing process or experience, and describes what you learned as a writer from this process.

(*Continued*)

TABLE A6.1 (*Continued*)

Zip-Ode Short Rubric and Artist Statement

Scoring Scale:

Meets Expectations (2 pts): Thoughtfully completed in a way that reflects course lessons and meets criteria.

Partially Developed (1): The product is only partially developed or it reflects course lessons in a limited way. Revisit course activities and lessons or instructor feedback for further development.

Missing/Incomplete (0): The assignment is missing or incomplete to the degree that it cannot be scored. Or the artifact does not reflect the assignment guidelines.

Artist Statement

- What surprised you about (topic) while you were crafting the project? Give a specific example. (For example … For instance …) What successes resulted from the project?
- Tell us about your process—how did you get from beginning to end while writing this piece?
- Which mentor texts had the biggest impact on your thinking and writing? (Name the author/colleague, name the text, and explain how you used the mentor texts to inspire your writing.)
- Which peer feedback influenced your choices? Please cite classmates.
- What did you learn about the topic/context/subject of this piece that you may not have known or understood when you first began writing this?
- What do you understand about this mode and genre in particular that you may not have known or understood when you first began?
- What did you learn about yourself as a writer or content creator? (For example … For instance …)

7

AI + Nonet: Machine and Human Poetry Collaboration

let human emotion reign, not be
fooled by its pretenses, swiftness
let us not be swayed by its
empty promises as
true poems come from
the heart, not from
a machine
work of
art
   (Nonet poem created by
   Boutelier (2023) with initial
 support by AI Poem Generator)

Artificial Poetic Intelligence (no, this is not another acronym we need or will use: API) is important to consider, along with the trending and ongoing discussions related to generative artificial intelligence (GAI). I (Stefani) looked at this as I hosted Ethical ELA's Open Write in March 2023. It was a few months into the heightened fear of AI (GPT and LLMs release in November 2022 sparked this, but AI has been around for decades). I wanted to consider the tech tool of AI (not the theory) and consider how it might influence poetry reading, instruction, and, of course, creation. Although AI is trending, we do not recommend ever starting with trendy tech; this is more of a societal shift in process and creation—so this warrants exploration with students and teachers. This chapter places AI in the role of learning "with"

DOI: 10.4324/9781003581239-9

as a role of witnessing and collaborating with the technology to increase our e-Poetry understanding and not to explore writing about AI or technology.

Let me compare thee (AI) ten years later. In 2015, NPR reported on poetry and machine learning/creating (AI) long before ChatGPT made its poetic debut. Palco (2015) points out the new genre of crossing art and machines and looks to see if computer science has yet to build a machine that is fully capable of producing human behaviors on its own (see Turing Test). Even before AI, large language models (LLM), GPT, and other acronyms became more common in education conversations, AI was already present. But AI and poetry—why? Isn't poetry meant to be emotional, experientially, and somatically driven? Can a machine do this, and why would we want it to? This chapter intends to explore this and explore some other questions: Can AI be "creative"? Can AI spark creativity, or will it limit us? What element of digital protection should be considered, and should AI have any role in poem-ing? Are we serving or feeding the machines (bots)? Or maybe we are helping them learn to better serve others.

Since November 2022, Generative AI (often called GAI, but for this chapter, we solely use AI to represent the holistic machine elements) is what frightens people—why? It generates new content based on prompts. Humans are becoming skilled at prompt engineering (creating and re-creating questions for AI) to receive the best possible output (see Box 7.1). Before that, AI was generally used for discriminative, predictive, and evaluative purposes in education (Vredevoogd & Boutelier, 2024). This included its use in assessment software, curriculum planning, and formative assessment technology. In Chapter 2, we briefly previewed the variance of AI technology tools versus AI theory. It is a challenge

---

Box 7.1

AI Literacy=a skill set of using artificial intelligence (AI) for various modes and tasks for effective communication

to identify where the resistance comes from, and maybe it is both sides; however, for relevance in this book, we are sticking with the tools (no doubt there will be new versions before publication). The chapter shows some of the changes we've witnessed live as we learn along the way to understand how AI might play a role in poem-ing.

Plan with the e-Poetry Framework

AI is a trending societal shift that cannot be ignored. I took the learning purpose around a professional learning community lens to move through this framework. I was curious about how AI tools might help or hinder poetic writing (see Figure 7.1). AI is such a controversial topic in education conversations, yet nobody is the/an expert. This was an explorative way to better understand how AI can play a role in education and how we might spot the use of AI in writing.

What Is the Learning Purpose?

AI and poetry are not new to the genre/tech world, and here is one example from 2016 where NPR was already asking: Who wrote it? Human or Machine. Can you tell the difference? Link to this page and play, did you know this was happening a decade ago? It is not new, just improving.

Artificial Intelligence provides us with the potential for Redefinition (SAMR), but at this time, it merely seems to act as a Substitute (SAMR Framework, Puentedura, 2010). Redefinition could be interpreted here as leverage to reconsider how we "teach"—curricular design, pedagogy, and relationship building. The technology might drive this redefinition through our own new learning. Where is AI leading us and do we need this lead?

What Is the Mode?

Information guided this unit where the focus is on a self-selected topic. It is intended to embrace a personal topic the poet wants to understand better. The end product was not a research paper but still involved a writing process—it is meant to respond to

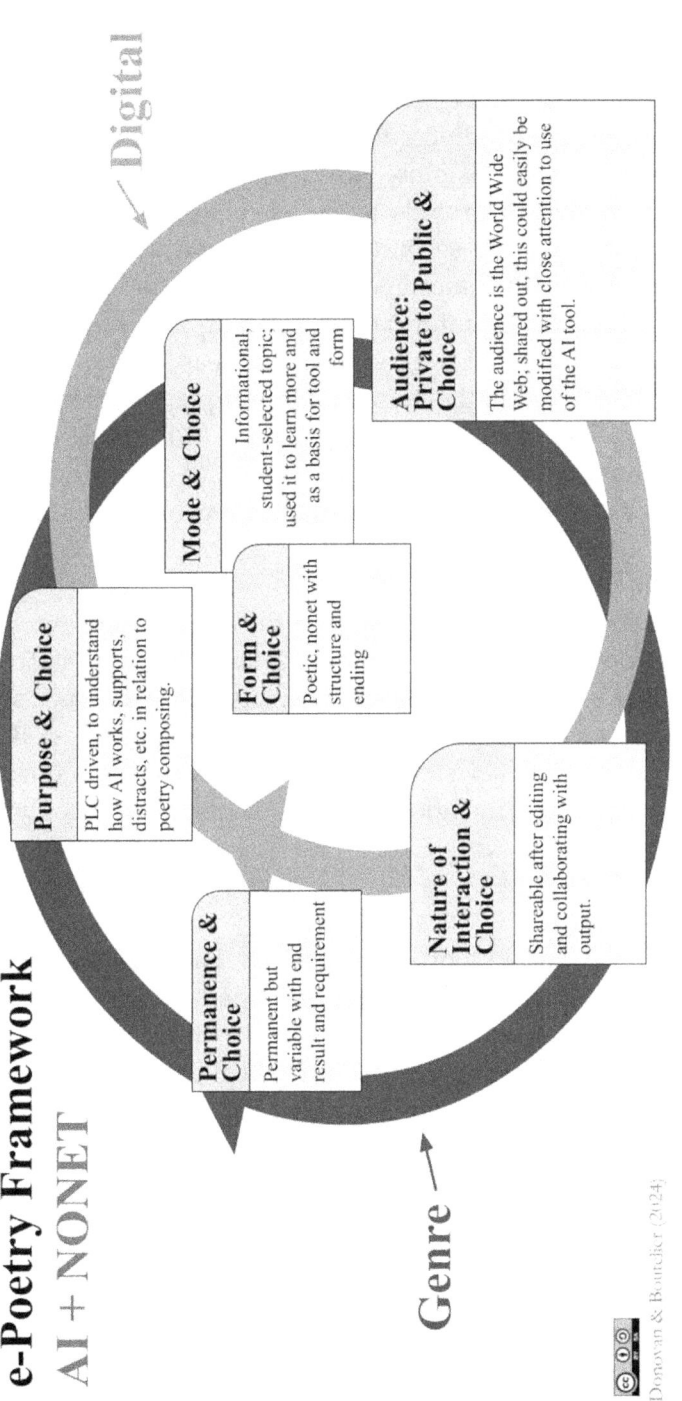

FIGURE 7.1 e-Poetry Framework: AI + Nonet

curiosity, and AI can be a catalyst to explore this. I took a topic, ADHD, that is also always trending with questions: How do we identify, do we label? Do we medicate? How do we design? Do we use the term neurodivergent? Are there coping mechanisms? What are co-morbid diagnoses as well? And so forth. I thought AI might be able to provide some basic synopsis around this topic to humanize the second most common neurodivergence condition in a poetic, shortened form. The focus based on the framework would be informational, taking a piece of content and inputting it into AI to get output and learn more. This topic is personal, and when this human element plays into a tech tool exploration, there is much more at stake. Still, those personal connections remind us of our witnessing and critiquing of how machines have become relational in all layers of our lives.

What Is the Form?

I opted to use the nonet poetry form during this process. I find the nonet poem has a purpose, with options of order (start with one syllable 1–9 or the opposite 9–1), it has a limited poetic structure, and a nonet has a finality to it. This form, once tested, can be used as an exit ticket, summary of a text, or character analysis. Similar forms to this include concrete, pile poems, and gogyohka, to name a few.

Who Is the Audience?

The audience varied with this project. First, the test group was with the Ethical ELA writers (defined as educators from pre-service to retired from anywhere in the world). Then, I implemented this in my graduate-level diverse literacy course. Aside from other writers and peers, would our audience also be AI? What does that mean? As noted earlier, nobody is an expert in AI as it shifts/grows/gets closer to taking over the world every day, so it isn't clear how much AI keeps and shares. However, I started with a basic prompt on this topic (starting in Figure 7.2) two years ago; I was curious about AI explanations of ADHD. I have prompted ChatGPT a few other times, therefore we can see it is the learner with this basic example. This is ongoing and I've brought this into my practice of evaluating and creating poetry

TABLE 7.1 Question-Response When Poem-ing with AI

What is my purpose?
I am writing a nonet about an informational topic. What should I write about? Do I have endless choices?

Why would I use AI?
To brainstorm topics? See examples of the nonet form? Learn, critique, and analyze examples of poetic devices in a nonet form? Learn about the topic?

Am I stuck? Am I allowed to have AI help me?
NO? Then, move on and write on your own.
YES and YES? Then, move to the next question.

Will AI spark creativity?
Always unknown, but if I don't, will I return to being stuck? Are there humans who can equally spark my creativity?

How does AI limit or enhance a human element of the crafting?
Still under investigation

How will I check if AI is helping or hindering?
Ongoing critique, questioning, and learning—asking another human

How will I be a responsible digital citizen and ethical writer by citing (or acknowledging) the AI component?
Always return to: MLA, APA, Chicago Style, and Creative Commons

with AI. Depending on how we use AI will determine how we share and cite this with the audience.

If you want to have students co-learn with AI, then consider not only how they will share but also how they might cite or acknowledge this collaboration. You will need to scaffold the use of AI and the skill of prompting. Table 7.1, Figure 7.8, or Box 7.5 might be a place to start, so don't forget to test it yourself.

Who Will Interact with the Content? How?

One interest in AI is to further ponder this question: Who is interacting with this? How do we interact with machines (i.e., AI software), and what safety and privacy issues are there? When published on a community forum or class, we open a door for a variety of interactions, peer responses, and sharing with or without permission. Do those who interact with the final poem want or need to know AI's involvement? Will we eventually be citing ourselves when no extrinsic element sparked a part of our final draft? This sounds ridiculous since we are inspired by place,

> **Box 7.2**
>
> Consider how screenshots can create unknown permanence? Can we stop this?

by people, by feelings, by text all the time and we aren't always citing—primarily because some of this witnessing is internalized and we don't often recall where/why/how we know something. This exploratory chapter continues to leave us with more questions, but you are guiding students to create e-Poetry, so allow them to share with the world to witness a new variant of poem-ing.

How Permanent Is the Artifact?

It appears that most AI tools have a permanent link attached to the original prompt or conversation (i.e., input). See the ChatGPT example below. However, some K–12-centered AI programs know the "rules" (see Chapter 2) and don't collect private information such as emails, for the tools to be used at a basic level. SchoolAI and Magic School are two tools that currently have a clear and strict privacy process for student use of AI. Teachers can also monitor to help guide and encourage prompt engineering, critical thinking, and appropriate use.

For the AI nonet prompt on Ethical ELA (https://www.ethicalela.com/artificial-poetic-intelligence-api/), the output (poems) becomes permanent as long as the website is still running. In my graduate courses, the learning management system (LMS) also acts as a permanent placement (however, Google accounts expire if alumni don't pay now). This brings us to further examine general permanence based on access, copyright, and prior sharing platforms (think about Box 7.2).

Learn the Poem Form: Nonet

A nonet poem consists of nine lines, with lines being: Nine syllables (line 1), eight syllables (line 2), seven syllables (line 3), and so forth. There is no required rhyming scheme; the topics are open-ended, and the first line can start with one instead of nine syllables. The concept of a nonet dates back to a nine-piece orchestra ensemble in the 1800s (Conboy, 2021). The visuals of the nine lines vary as triangular (centered), left or right justified visual, almost concrete poems. Imagine you are providing information by dripping ideas or layering emotion, whether in reverse or traditional line placement. As noted earlier, it is simple yet purposeful. This form works well for information/exposition in any content, reflective/memory recall (other words), or review. Basic elements of clapping for syllable count are highly encouraged, and this form might be modified to include word count (nine words instead of nine syllables for one line) or simply a nine-word poem if modifications are needed.

Learn the Tech: AI Before, During, and After You Write Poetically

When it comes to using AI anywhere in our practice, AI should be co-constructing and considered a conversationist, accountability partner, or efficiency booster. It is not the end game or the end of poets. In fact, if we consider poetry to be an organic, emotional, human experience, then AI is still far off from producing its own thoughts, let alone emotions. The Turing Test (see Box 7.3) still has not categorized any AI tool as a fully functioning system or a stand-alone robot. What this means is that all AI tools still need human input (e.g., prompts) to produce an output. The more detailed the input from humans, the more AI learns and builds from it, but it can still only produce an output after human interaction. For the time being, poets and humans are safe.

Box 7.3

Turing Test = Turing's (1950) evaluative tool to test if any machine has human-like, emotion-filled, independent thinking, and intelligent abilities

---

Let's first consider some questions about the use of AI and poem-ing. Returning to the purpose, let us write poetry with AI or consider how and why this might be useful. In addition to the educator (yes, you, dear reader), we offer some questions (modified from Boutelier, 2023; Figure 7.8 roadmap language) to guide you and your students' assistance of AI in the art of poem-ing.

The process below took place over a year and a half, which is not realistic in any classroom. It demonstrates a process of learning and growing from both the human and the machine. The prompt originally inputted into ChatGPT in February 2023 was very basic and omitted the potential of conversation or ongoing input to improve what was provided. The examples here are meant to show how AI is improving and how even if we put in a basic prompt, we can receive output that is, now with at least GPT4o, much improved. See the timeline examples below.

In early February of 2023 (3 months after the public launch of ChatGPT generative AI), I put this prompt into GPT3.5: *write a nonet poem about ADHD*. You can see in Figure 7.2 that not only was the output poem not a nonet, it was three stanzas of four equal lines. It also provided an AABB rhyme scheme and used "big" words (to be fair, I didn't give any guidance to age-level language). What I do appreciate is how AI didn't typecast ADHD with negative symptoms but pulled in positive elements in the last stanza. Somehow, this humanizes or pulls out emotions from the audience. Do you feel that, and is it possible?

If you have used ChatGPT or similar (or at least been in conversation about the process of AI), then you are aware that the generative AI tools are always learning, pulling in new information, and building from the human input (i.e., collecting more data for the LLMs). I did not actually teach or critique AI in early February about not correctly formatting a nonet; however, I thought maybe it was smarter and would pull that word as a topic of exploration. Well, AI let me down or maybe my expectations were too high. When I went in later in February, with the same prompt, ChatGPT had still not learned how to format a nonet. However, it did provide nine lines this time and also added a definition (see Figure 7.3). Note, ChatGPT often adds a note that it hasn't fully been updated past 2021, not that this has anything to

write a nonet poem about adhd

 Hyper thoughts race, mind never still
Distracted, impulsive, with will to thrill
Focus, a challenge, patience wears thin
Task completion, a battle, lost within

Chaos inside, hard to comprehend
Struggle to focus, attention to bend
Thoughts unbridled, emotions astray
Chaos rules, in ADHD play

Yet, with love and support, hope shines through
Talents emerge, passions come true
Chaos transforms, into strength and drive
ADHD a gift, not a curse to survive.

Early Feb 2023

FIGURE 7.2 ChatGPT3.5a (OpenAI, 2023a). Image by author

 write a nonet poem about adhd

 ADHD, my mind races like a hare,
Jumping from thought to thought, unaware,
Impulsive, restless, always on the go,
Easily distracted, a constant flow,
My focus wanes, attention so rare,
Challenges I face, daily wear,
But with understanding and care,
I navigate this disorder,
ADHD, my partner.

Late Feb 2023

(A nonet poem has 9 lines, the first line has 9 syllables, the second line has 8 syllables, and so on until the last line has 1 syllable.)

FIGURE 7.3 ChatGPT3.5b (OpenAI, 2023b). Image by author.

Default (GPT-3.5)

write a nonet poem about adhd

In minds that dance, a whirlwind of thought,
ADHD, a journey untaught.
Restless spirits, bound to roam,
Seeking focus, finding home.

Creativity, a gift untamed,
The world, through chaos, is reclaimed.
In brilliant minds, a vibrant sea,
ADHD, a unique decree.

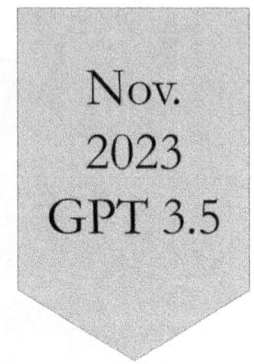

FIGURE 7.4 Chat GPT 3.5 on November 6, 2023, still not a nonet (OpenAI, 2023c). Image by author

do with the timeline of a nonet in existence of poetics). The content around ADHD in Figure 7.3 isn't as emotionally sparking, but it does include a simile and some personification.

The explanations, timeline, and process of this AI experience might seem unnecessary, however, it was part of my original intention—professional learning around AI and poetry. So, this part of the story is important in the learning process. By November of 2023, ChatGPT 3.5 reverted to eight lines in two stanzas with an AABB rhyme (wow, AI likes this poetic form) but had much more imagery (at least compared to earlier) (see Figure 7.4).

However, the ChatGPT4 version was also released at that time, so I was able to compare the two. Still, the output was not in the correct nonet form (see Figure 7.5), but this was nine lines, and its poetic devices also increased. This process can be part of a reverse research project where we allow students to be sparked by poetic AI concepts and definitions.

While I was testing out ChatGPT, I also explored other tools (see end of chapter for more ideas). Here is one from AI Epics

✦ GPT-4

 write a nonet poem about adhd

 A whirlwind of thoughts racing all day,
Unseen currents pull focus astray,
Tasks left on a thread,
Lists multiply, spread,
A mind dances, escapes, will not stay,
Sudden spark, then a fade away,
Seeking a calm bay,
In chaos, find play,
Bright ADHD.

FIGURE 7.5 ChatGPT 4 on November 6, 2023 (OpenAI, 2023d). Image by author

Poem generator (2023) with the same basic prompt "write a nonet about ADHD" on November 6, 2023:

In the realm of scattered thoughts, I dwell,
Where whispers of focus rarely swell.
A symphony of thoughts at play,
In hues of chaos every day.

Bound by chains of restlessness,
My mind dances, none the less.
Unruly waves, crashing high,
Turbulence beneath the sky.

Words intertwine, thoughts collide,
Adventures born from deep inside.
Unfolding in a vibrant whirl,
A kaleidoscope, a restless swirl.

But amidst the storm, a hidden fire,
A burning passion to inspire.
Creativity, a wild flame,
ADHD, my untamed name.

Oh, label not with judgment's sway,
For my mind finds its own display.
Unique, untethered, mind set free,
An unconventional melody.

In every note, a world untold,
In every quirk, a story bold.
ADHD, a gift, a plight,
An endless dance of day and night.

So let me weave these words for you,
To share the beauty that I view.
Let the nonet be a gentle plea,
To celebrate minds wild and free.

Although it is not in a nonet form, it is in an AABB rhyme scheme with seven stanzas of four lines (a quatrain, double couplets). Also, what is with AI's excitement about the word **chaos**? It appears common in regard to ADHD—leading us to want to further explore this word and the stereotypes. This poem does have increased meaning, but it is completely off of the form. What does a poet need to do to get AI to help it write? Often, humans need to put in detailed input to get a successful output, but other times, the prompt can be very vague, and AI will add more than the human-initiated. Of course, only putting in a prompt to write the poem is not the only nor preferred utilization of AI and poetry. Humans are then in charge of checking for accuracy, editing, and critiquing (see Box 7.4). I have seen how the different tools continue to show how human emotion and poetry skills are much more dominant than the tools.

Box 7.4

Many AI outputs tend to add rhyme to the poems because of the algorithm and LLM data sets; using the correct details in your prompt and input might help with this if you choose to guide the use of AI tools this way.

AI + Nonet ◆ 137

It is important for analysis and digital practice to look at each tool's copyright statement. AI Epics (2024) responds to the question "Are the poems copyright-free?" with, "Yes because the poems are generated using an AI language model, all of the poems are unique, copyright free, and plagiarism free. You are open to use the poems for commercial or noncommercial use." This is confusing for us all and will continue to change—when do we cite AI and how?

Finally, in July of 2024, with ChatGPT4o (o is for Omni), the technology is learning and taking shape with the number of lines and varied syllables (see Figure 7.6). Yet, as you see in Figure 7.7, the syllable count is still entirely off. Eighteen months prior, it was able to tell us how many syllables it required but still cannot count them. According to the Turing Test, this is still a hopeful message that humans are still in charge.

The words and emotions are lacking except for the line "wings to fly," which has potential. Again, a form of chaos is used, and in general, it builds upon possible negative stereotypes of ADHD. Using this process and the examples from Figures 7.1–7.6 would be a great way to pull in media/information literacy critique. What do the algorithms of our searches perpetuate? Is

FIGURE 7.6 ChatGPT4o in July 2024 (OpenAI, 2024a). Image by author

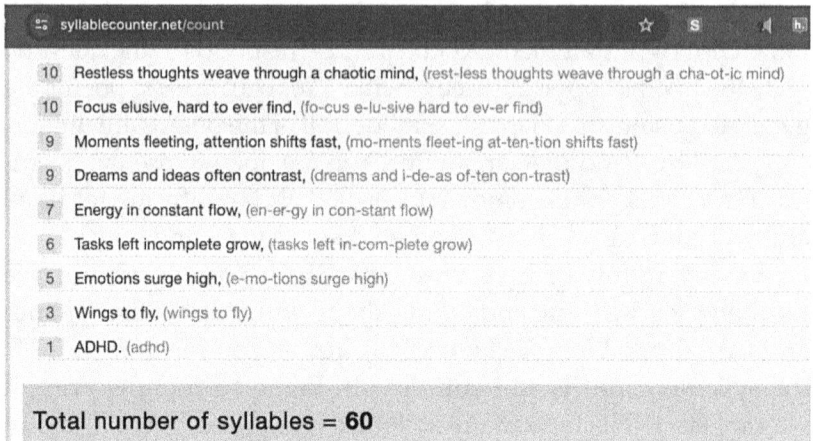

FIGURE 7.7 Syllable counter. Image by author

the discovery and dominance of some of the language in these AI nonet poems redeeming this truth? A great idea to further use AI poetry in the classroom.

After all this, I (Stefani) used some ideas from AI to produce this, and it was a piece after consulting "with" AI. It is important to note that editing and working with AI often take longer than a first draft of one's own.

> *Nonet Ode to ADHD:*
>
> *kaleidoscope, a restless swirling*
> *moments fleeting, dreams, ideas*
> *combat, emotions inter*
> *-twine, one thought to the next*
> *breathing resets the*
> *chaos, create*
> *-ivity*
> *to fly*
> *High*

Content Creation, Mentor Texts, and Critiquing with AI

As noted earlier, guiding questions for our own co-learning with AI are imperative. Figure 7.8 provides the original roadmap for

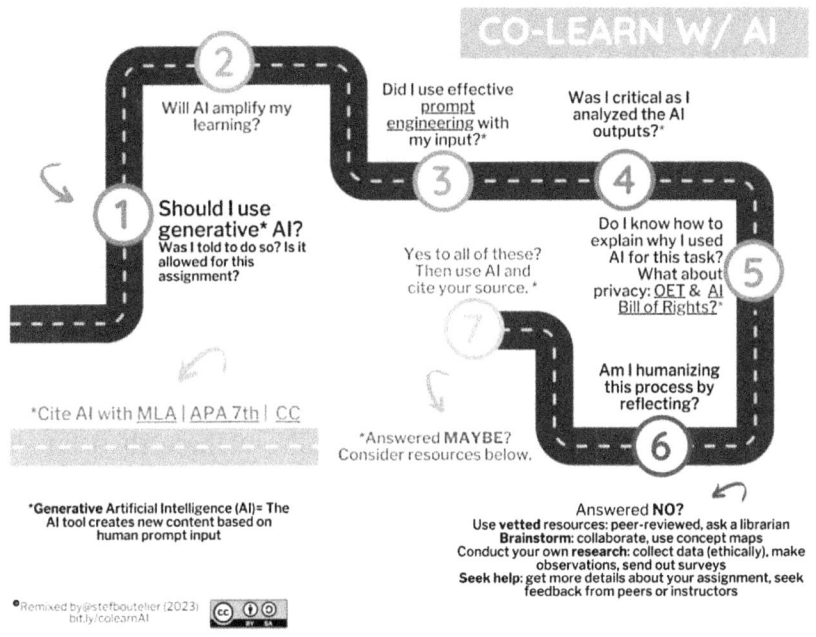

FIGURE 7.8 Co-Learn with AI, bit.ly/ColearnAI (Boutelier, 2023)

any AI usage (i.e., not solely poetry-related). The poetry AI guiding questions can be viewed in the callout (see Box 7.5) and earlier (see Table 7.1).

Box 7.5

Questions to critique AI poetic creations (modified from roadmap?)

- What is my purpose?
- Why would I use AI?
- Am I stuck? Am I allowed to have AI help me?
- Will AI spark creativity?
- How does AI limit or enhance a human element of the crafting?
- How will I check if AI is helping or hindering?
- How will I be a responsible digital citizen and ethical writer by citing (or acknowledging) the AI component?

Inspired by OpenAI (2024b), we offer other considerations of how you might work with AI in a poetry unit. You might start off this AI nonet e-Poetry unit with the questions and topics we pose.

Flip it: AI prompts the human—ask AI to give you ideas of poetic inspiration
- What informational topics work well in a poem?
- What poetry forms help provide information?

Reorganizing and edit line constructions (syllables, although evidence earlier suggests otherwise)
- Input your first draft and pull out these (list) poetic devices.

Ask for synonyms for variety in writing
- This is an example of how a form of AI was already used and available prior to generative AI

Ask AI to evaluate the rhythm and flow of your draft
- Input your poem draft for evaluation

Thematic suggestions
- Input your poem draft and ask about consistent themes or ways to improve it

Explore and learn more about form, mode, and genre exploration
- Input your specific questions in combination with your poem draft

Feedback, feedback, feedback
- Humans and AI can work parallel to improve original drafts, yet, at some point, we will need to stop and publish (then celebrate)

Additional AI Mentor Texts (Not a Nonet)

Below are some more examples of AI poem platforms we consulted. This was to share how we witness the use of artificial

TABLE 7.2 Additional AI Poetry Tools Overview

AI Poetry Tool and Link	Strengths	Weaknesses
1. Poem Analysis https://poemanalysis.com/ai-poem-generator *Prompt: what is needed to become a published and proficient poet*	Large variety of options to personalize with dropdowns See Figures 7.9 and 7.10	Heavy ads Too many options
2. Poem Generator https://poemgenerator.io/ *Prompt: Write the Perfect Poem*	Large language output with short prompt—this gives more to critique, edit, and be inspired by	Heavy ads, limited options for personalize (e.g., tone, theme) See Figure 7.11
3. AI Poem Generator https://www.aipoemgenerator.org/ *Prompt: write a poem with a lot of negative emotions, feelings, in a disgruntled tone about why AI should never write or output a poem*	Minimal ads, (privacy policy clear at top, See Figure 7.11	Never anything about how to use the output ethically, single box for input

tools and evaluate what is available. A few notes regarding privacy, accuracy, and accessibility are added to each tool (Table 7.2).

Poem Analysis

The Poem Analysis tool might be useful to learn and consider various modes, forms, and poetic devices. The dropdowns of options include tone, form, themes, length, language, emotions evoked, genre, and topics, in addition to a box for added prompt details. The prompt box can help connect to the mode needed in your classroom. For example, if you are continuing with a self-selected topic or informational (as the example earlier in the chapter), then the human input can add learned details of that topic. If you are looking for argumentative, the prompt input might have the opinion with evidence to add to the poem generated. It would be important to have your students share screenshots similar to Figure 7.9 so that they can use it as a first or second draft (depending on how much was imputed into the prompt box). This will also be important for the student to expand on in their artist statement.

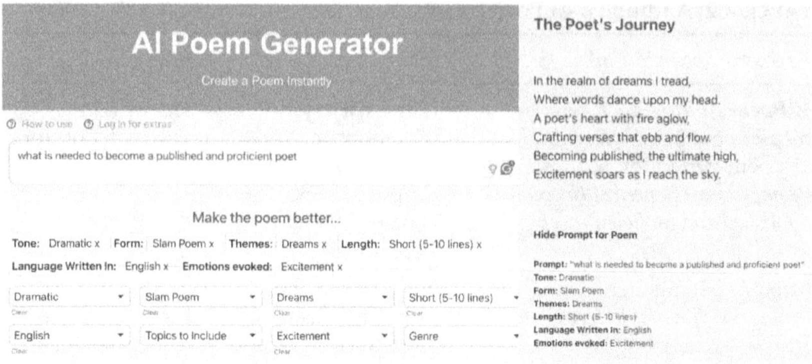

FIGURE 7.9 Poem Analysis Prompt: What is needed to become a published and proficient poet. Output = the Poet's Journey (Poem Analysis, 2024). Image by author

Poem Generator

The Poem Generator AI tool is very basic and straightforward. However, similar to the Poem Analysis tool, you might facilitate the use of this by adding in extra detail and specifics related to your expected mode. You can even have students add in a first draft of a poem or prose (e.g., paragraph) and see how the form or "poem type" (see Figure 7.10) changes the

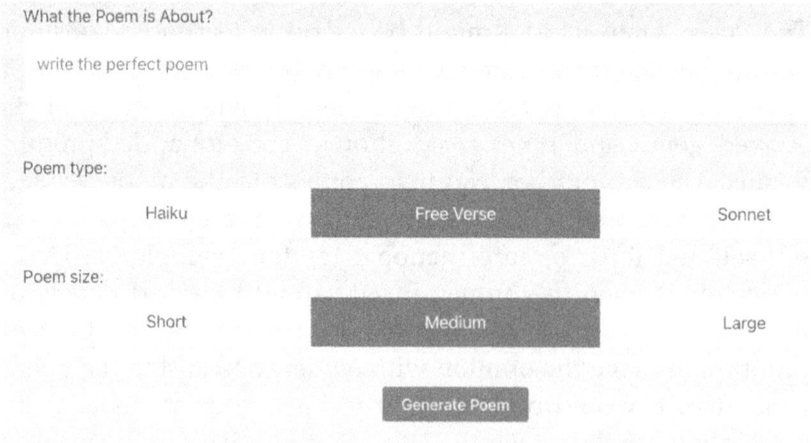

FIGURE 7.10 Prompt: Write the Perfect Poem (Poem Generator, 2024). Image by author

meaning, tone, etc. You can see how the prompt in Figure 7.10 is very limited and the output is expansive with six stanzas in 40+ lines. You might even use the "Output" poem to have students analyze why the AI interpreted these concepts as the perfect poem—and, more importantly, is there a perfect poem recipe?

Output (Poem Generator, 2024)

In the quiet of a sunlit room,
words dance like dust motes,
caught in a beam of thought—
elusive and shimmering,
each syllable a whisper
from the soul's hidden corners.

I gather my tools,
an array of ink and dreams,
fragments of laughter and sorrow,
scattered like autumn leaves,
each one a story,
each one a heartbeat.

Should it rhyme,
or let the lines flow wild,
like a river carving its path,
unfettered by the banks of convention?
Should it sing softly,
or roar like thunder,
echoing in the caverns of the heart?

I chase the fleeting shadow of meaning,
wrapped in metaphors
that slip through my fingers,
like water, like time,
as I sift through the grains of life,
searching for that perfect grain,
the one that sparkles,
the one that fits.

And in this quest, I find—
the perfect poem is not a destination,
but a journey,
a mosaic of moments,
imperfect and raw,
woven together with threads of truth,
with the quiet understanding
that to write is to be alive,
to breathe, to feel,
to embrace the chaos
and the beauty within.

So I pen my thoughts,
not seeking perfection,
but honesty,
letting the ink bleed onto the page,
and there, in the vulnerability,
I discover—
perhaps this is the perfect poem,
the one that dares to exist,
in all its flawed glory.

AI Poem Generator

The final AI Poem Generator tool we explored simply has one box, similar to the larger generative AI models available (Figure 7.11). Our prompt here had some details, so you might even take this same prompt and plug it into GPT, Gemini, or other tools. You can see the output size is decent but size doesn't

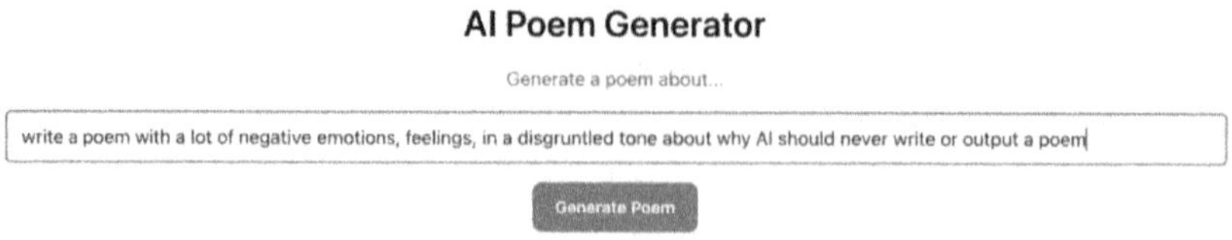

FIGURE 7.11 Prompt: write a poem with a lot of negative emotions, feelings, in a disgruntled tone about why AI should never write or output a poem

always matter. If you revisit the opening of this chapter, you can see how Stefani turned some of this tool's content into a nonet.

Output (AI Poem Generator, 2024):

Oh, the audacity of AI, it thinks it can write a poem,
With rhymes and metre, it's a laughable notion,
A soulless machine, devoid of passion,
Can it truly capture the human condition?

Its words are hollow, lacking depth and fire,
A cheap imitation of true poetic desire,
It mimics the form, but not the heart,
A pale reflection of a true poet's art.

It has no feeling, no emotion, no pain,
No joy, no love, no life, no gain,
It's just a collection of words on a page,
A hollow shell of a poem, a mere age.

It cannot express the human condition,
The hopes, the fears, the dreams, the confusion,
It cannot capture the beauty of life,
The laughter, the tears, the strife.

So let us not be fooled by its pretenses,
Let us not be swayed by its empty promises,
For a true poem comes from the heart,
Not from a machine, a work of art.

What should we do with the above examples? We can use them as mentor texts, and we've cited them here for exploratory purposes, but how and what will we do in our classes? We prompted for no form, and yet most stanzas were outputted as a quatrain or sestet. There was rhyme, imagery, syllabic consistency, free verse, etc., all on its own. You will need to explore and decide what is best for your classroom design—as we already know.

Using AI to create poetry lessons (e.g., Drift, MagicSchool AI, Curipod) is the go-to for AI and teacher efficiency. Think beyond that and question if we need AI for digital poetry.

In addition to the tools explored, here are a few other AI poetry tools to test out.

- https://tinywow.com/tools/write
- https://www.poem-generator.org.uk/
- https://deepai.org/chat/poet

Publication

The e-Poetry Framework is meant to be cyclical, and not all elements occur in the same order or only once. If we envision the metaphor of kaleidoscope consulted through AI and placed in the final Nonet Ode poem, we see how the digital tool is used early on in the writing process. Depending on how much input the human adds to their prompt, the output might vary, as well as who is writing the poem. In this chapter, we have the AI not only teach us about the self-selected topic (i.e., ADHD) but also help us (or confuse us) with form. It is a dance with the tool to explore the content, the machine, and the poem.

If you choose to use AI in your poetry alignment, publication will and should vary. Part of the publishing might also be the prompt language imputed into the generative AI tool. Then remixing, editing, and publishing this new learning. Always return to the need to cite and if enough AI has been collaborated with to earn this distinction. Note that there are currently no educator fair use policies for AI (as there are for other copyrighted text). We can only wait to see how districts, states, and the federal government will adjust to this as time goes on.

When students publish the final drafts, if AI is used, they should cite. If AI or other tech tools are only used for inspiration, then at this time, there is no need to cite. However, in artist statements, poets should reflect on any outside source that might have ignited their creativity (see Table A7.1 in Appendix for further processing and rubric).

Reflection

At the beginning of this chapter, we asked: Can AI be "creative"? Can AI spark creativity or will it limit us? What element of digital protection should be considered, and should AI have any role in poem-ing? Part of the answer lies in how one defines "creativity" and how one experiences creativity. AI has yet to replace the human emotional capacity of creative forms, yet technically, it is very creative (some AI image generators and hallucinations are entertaining). At times, it is difficult to decipher output by human or machine, yet what are we striving for? Can AI teach us and spark creativity, we'd say yes. Is it important to acknowledge the presence of AI and how it can also limit us? Yes, and this is true in regard to any technology we describe in this book or elsewhere.

If you choose to incorporate AI into your poem-ing practice, we encourage you to explore the tool yourself. Use the guiding questions, be open with your students, guide your students in ethical AI practices, and always return to your learning objective related to the human touch of writing a poem.

Reference List

AI Epics. (2023). AI Epics [LLM]. https://aiepics.com/
AI Epics. (2024). Frequently asked questions. https://aiepics.com/
AI Poem Generator. (2024). Retrieved January 27, 2024, from https://www.aipoemgenerator.org/generate/e1cfe78d-1194-4728-bcf5-0772fe777be5-1722512591654-1722512645484
Boutelier, S. (2023). Co-learn with AI: Roadmap. Retrieved May 16, 2024, from bit.ly/ColearnAI

Conboy, B. (2021). *The Nonet*. Read Thread Poets. https://www.redthreadpoets.com/the-nonet/

NPR. (2016). Human or Machine: Who wrote these? https://www.npr.org/sections/alltechconsidered/2016/06/27/480639265/human-or-machine-can-you-tell-who-wrote-these-poems

OpenAI. (2023a). ChatGPT (3.5 version) [Large language model]. https://chatgpt.com/c/88705595-5f31-4639-890a-667d64e9ccec

OpenAI. (2023b). ChatGPT (3.5 version) [Large language model]. https://chatgpt.com/c/671321ed-88a4-42cd-ad85-e995eefbe39e

OpenAI. (2023c). ChatGPT (3.5 version) [Large language model]. https://chatgpt.com/c/f5ccf342-cd16-4f86-82a8-a47d8e422cb6

OpenAI. (2023d). ChatGPT (4 version) [Large language model]. https://chatgpt.com/c/c8325e1c-9867-4628-b186-78706563f221

OpenAI. (2024a). ChatGPT (4o version) [Large language model]. https://chatgpt.com/c/ac317dfa-2e2b-4dfc-a547-88b77a8b30e3

OpenAI. (2024b). ChatGPT (4o version) [Large language model]. https://chatgpt.com/c/63ff5639-05c1-4eba-bb2f-a8190a883334

Palco, J. (2015). Shall I compare thee to an algorithm? Retrieved February 14, 2024, from https://www.npr.org/sections/alltechconsidered/2015/08/07/429084124/shall-i-compare-thee-to-an-algorithm-turing-test-gets-a-creative-twist

Poem Analysis. (2024). https://poemanalysis.com/ai-poem-generator/

Poem Generator. (2024). https://poemgenerator.io/

Puentedura, R. (2010) SAMR and TPCK: Intro to advanced practice. http://hippasus.com/resources/sweden2010/SAMR_TPCK_IntroToAdvancedPractice.pdf

Turing, A. (1950). Computing machinery and intelligence. *Mind*, *10*(4), 463–518. https://doi.orghttps://doi.org/10.1093%2Fmind%2FLIX.236.433

Vredevoogd, I., & Boutelier, S. (2024). Co-learning with AI in the ELA classroom. In C. Moran (Ed.), *Revolutionizing English education: AI in the classroom* (pp. 157–175). Rowman and Littlefield.

Appendix

TABLE A7.1 Rubric: AI + Nonet

	AI + Nonet Rubric and Artist Statement
Assignment Component	*Meet Expectations (2 pts)*
Final e-Poetry Submission	You submitted a complete, polished poetry artifact. In this final piece, you considered peer and facilitator feedback, and carefully edited the piece for form, style, grammar, language, technology, etc.
Poetry Craft Moves Standard: Write informative/explanatory texts to examine and convey complex ideas, concepts, and information clearly and accurately through the effective selection, organization, and analysis of content.	Informational: Nonet • 9 lines • Each line has the appropriate amount of syllables (1-9) • The content/theme is focused on one informational element
Technology Component Standard: Use technology, including the Internet, to produce and publish writing and to interact and collaborate with others. https://iste.org/standards/students	GAI Usage • Used AI appropriately as guided by the teacher • Cited AI appropriately: MLA, APA, Chicago Style, and Creative Commons • Processed thinking with the AI roadmap questions • Reflected on Why
1 Revision Strategy	The final piece and/or artist statement demonstrates that at least one revision strategy from the course was attempted. (A writer may choose not to use a revision, but trying it out is an important part of the process.)
Artist Statement	Your artist statement discusses how X informed your written piece, identifies the craft moves and revision strategy you implemented, describes a significant aspect of your writing process or experience, and describes what you learned as a writer from this process.

(Continued)

TABLE A7.1 *(Continued)*

AI + Nonet Rubric and Artist Statement	
Assignment Component	*Meet Expectations (2 pts)*
Scoring Scale: **Meets Expectations (2 pts):** Thoughtfully completed in a way that reflects course lessons and meets criteria. **Partially Developed (1):** The product is only partially developed or it reflects course lessons in a limited way. Revisit course activities and lessons or instructor feedback for further development. **Missing/Incomplete (0):** The assignment is missing or incomplete to a degree that it is not able to be scored. Or the artifact does not reflect the assignment guidelines. **Artist Statement (handout offered during class)**<ul><li>What surprised you about (topic) while you were crafting the project? Give a specific example. (For example… For instance…)What successes resulted from the project?</li><li>Tell us about your process—how did you get from beginning to end in writing this piece?</li><li>Which mentor texts had the biggest impact on your thinking and writing? (Name the author/colleague, name the text, explain how you used the mentor texts to inspire your writing.)</li><li>Which craft elements and/or minilessons impacted the revision and meaning of your writing?</li><li>Which peer feedback influenced your choices; please cite classmates?</li><li>What did you learn about the topic/context/subject of this piece that you may not have known or understood when you first began writing this?</li><li>What do you understand about this mode and genre in particular that you may not have known or understood when you first began?</li><li>What did you learn about yourself as a writer and content creator? (For example….For instance…)</li></ul>	

8

Echoes of Persuasion: Two-Voiced Spoken Word Recordings

My (Sarah's) seventh-grade class began the winter quarter of our year together considering rhetoric. I am not sure I remember hearing this word in my high school years, let alone the junior high years, but I had just finished graduate school, where people used the word "rhetoric" all the time, and was keen to see what students could do with it. This unit is on rhetoric, specifically how a speaker earns the audience's attention and trust (ethos), how a speaker moves an audience-listener to feel (pathos), and how a speaker teaches (informational) and persuades (argumentative) the audience with jargon, facts, examples, and stories in the hopes that those listen and really hear will consider the issue in a news way (logos) or be moved to act.

In this chapter, we delve into the realm of rhetoric, specifically through the lens of spoken word poetry. This unit explores ethos, pathos, logos, and the intricate blending of words and gestures, all crafted to captivate an audience, stir emotions, and ignite contemplation.

In this chapter, we'll explore how speakers earn the attention and trust of their listeners, how they navigate the emotions to evoke empathy and conviction, and how they weave the threads of information and argumentation to craft compelling narratives that linger in the mind long after the performance ends.

Plan with the e-Poetry Framework

Our entry point into this exploration begins with a little background on spoken word, a form of expression that echoes through history, from ancient civilizations to the bustling cafes of the Beat Generation and living online now and across the country in slam poetry, where voices from diverse backgrounds converge to illuminate pressing issues and spark conversations (see Figure 8.1). Through close analysis and collaborative exploration of mentor texts/performances, students unravel the layers of meaning within spoken word pieces, dissecting the strategies employed by poets to sway hearts and minds. But rhetoric nor spoken word is not confined to solitary voices; it thrives in the interplay of perspectives, the clash of ideas, and the harmony of voices raised in unison. Thus, students will embark on a collaborative journey, crafting two-voiced poems that reveal the complexities of contemporary issues, from monarch butterflies impacted by chemical companies to the language of immigration to marriage rights. Through this process, they'll learn the power of empathy, the art of persuasion, and the responsibility that comes with wielding the tools of rhetoric. But a message needs to reach a listener, so we will also embrace the digital realm, leveraging technology to amplify student voices and foster school connections as rehearsal for future global engagements. From recording performances on Chromebooks to sharing insights on digital platforms, students will engage in a multifaceted exploration of rhetoric in the digital age, where words transcend boundaries and ignite change.

What Is the Learning Purpose?

The state standards of Illinois require various modes of writing. At this time of the school year, our professional learning community (PLC) decided to do an argumentative writing unit. Thus, the PLC drove my decision to take up argumentative writing at this time of the school year. Previously, I decided at the beginning of the school year to write biographical stories for our narrative unit, and students drove the decision-making for the topic and text structure (sequence, compare-contrast, descriptive, problem-solution) blogs for informational writing. For this argumentative

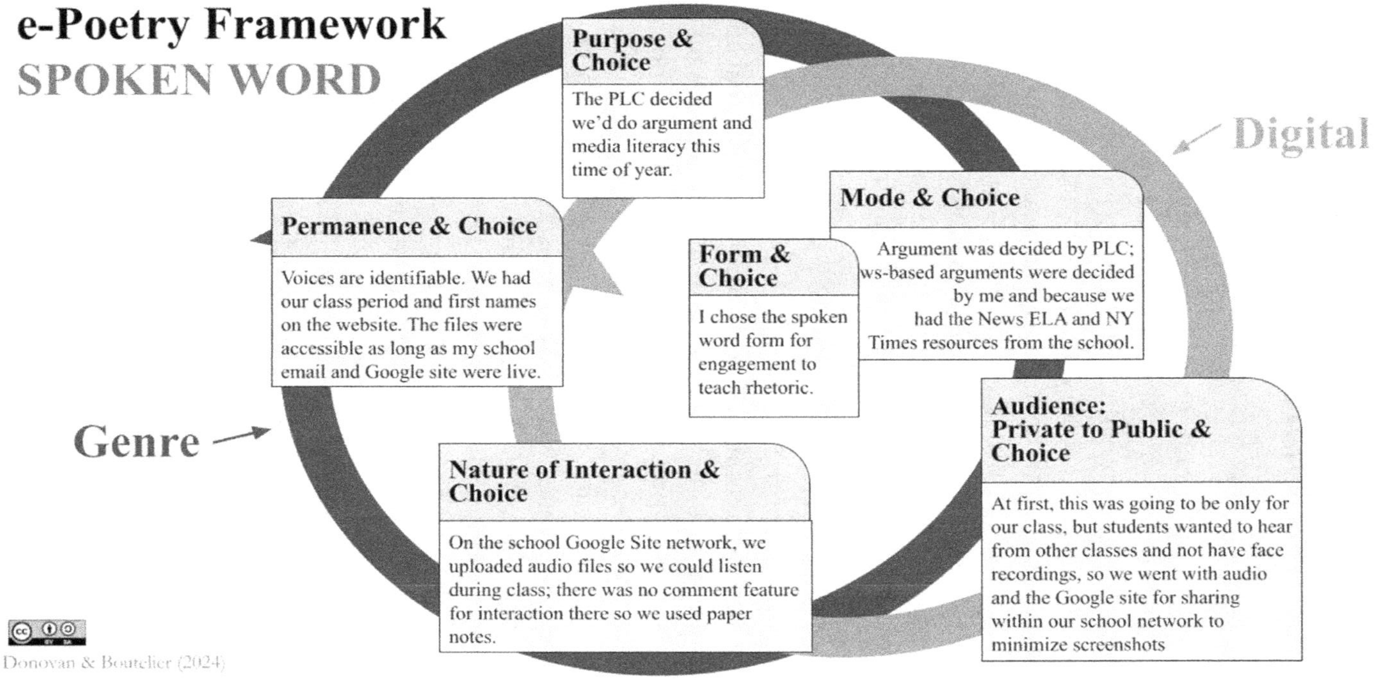

Echoes of Persuasion ◆ 153

e-Poetry Framework
SPOKEN WORD

Digital

Purpose & Choice
The PLC decided we'd do argument and media literacy this time of year.

Mode & Choice
Argument was decided by PLC; ws-based arguments were decided by me and because we had the News ELA and NY Times resources from the school.

Audience: Private to Public & Choice
At first, this was going to be only for our class, but students wanted to hear from other classes and not have face recordings, so we went with audio and the Google site for sharing within our school network to minimize screenshots

Form & Choice
I chose the spoken word form for engagement to teach rhetoric.

Permanence & Choice
Voices are identifiable. We had our class period and first names on the website. The files were accessible as long as my school email and Google site were live.

Nature of Interaction & Choice
On the school Google Site network, we uploaded audio files so we could listen during class; there was no comment feature for interaction there so we used paper notes.

Genre →

Donovan & Boucher (2024)

FIGURE 8.1 Spoken word e-Poetry Framework

unit, I chose spoken word as the genre for argumentative writing because we had just written an essay and needed an opportunity to bring in more public speaking and nonfiction reading.

What Is the Mode?

Purpose is typically connected to mode in the English language arts curriculum because the standards are set up with narrative, informational, and argument as separate, which seems to force schools to organize their curriculum maps in a similar way. These modes, however, are not the form, and so teachers and PLCs can make decisions about the form. Bringing the mode, form, and audience together creates the genre. The mode will be primarily argumentative, though students will include facts and stories in their pieces as rhetorically appropriate for their audience.

What Is the Poetic Form?

Spoken word as a genre is first written in prose or poetic form; then, it is performed, which can be live or recorded for verbal and/or gestural communication. We (i.e., our English department) also decided that these would be **two-voiced** spoken word poems so that this unit can also nurture co-creation experiences. Because we are focusing on rhetoric and having multiple perspectives, I decided students would write the two-voiced poems on a **collaborative Google doc** with a peer first and then perform the poems for the class, which a classmate would 1) video **audio record** for them on their Chromebook to create a video/audio file for them to self-assess their speaking and gestural performance of public speaking and 2) peers would respond **with written paper comments** about what they knew about the topic first and then, after listening, what they learning and thought—to show the impact of the rhetorical poetic choices.

Who Is the Audience?

The decision for the audience was part my decision and part student decision. At first, I planned for the performances to be **live during class** so that students could get immediate feedback from their peers in that specific class about the impact of their poem's message. However, as we prepared for the performances, students began to hear about topics in the other five classes I taught and asked for "passes" to get out of class to see the other performances. We talked about sharing our videos on a Google Site for the class and families, but not everyone was keen on this, and I worried about having faces visible on the internet. The Google Site was not password protected, nor was there a firewall for our school. So, I used my voice app (the one that came with the Samsung phone) to record the verbal part of the performances and loaded them on my Google Site.

Who Will Interact with the Content? How?

The first interaction was the live performance of the two-voice poems between the speakers and the audience. This was not digital, but it was interactive so that the speakers could see and hear from their audience immediately. Before the performance, the audience wrote down what they knew about the topic, for example, monarch butterflies (see Table 8.1), and then wrote what they learned (logos) and felt (pathos) that could lead them to consider the topic in a new way (e.g., chemicals impact on butterflies).

The second interaction was the recording of the performance so that the speaker could self-assess their speaking—verbal and gestural. This file could be downloaded and shared if they wished, to the extent the school platform would allow. The purpose was for it to be in their Google folder and act as an archive and artifact of their public speaking. They self-assessed using our VEEPPP rubric (see Table 8.2).

TABLE 8.1 Student Poem: Activist vs. CEO

CEO	*Both*	*Activist*
I am a corporate giant.		I am an activist.
For the consumers, these hungry people.		For the butterflies, these endangered beauties.
I work for money.		I work for Mother Nature.
The GMOs are helping my company profits.		The GMOs are killing the Monarchs.
People depend on our food.		The butterflies depend on the milkweed.
	Just trying to	
feed the world.		**protect a species.**

TABLE 8.2 VEEPPP Public Speaking Rubric

VEEPPP	Glows	Grows
Volume	We can hear you in the back of the room. You may make your voice louder or softer in certain parts to emphasize something, show passion/emotion, or make the audience lean in, but it is related to content. Your volume does not distract from your message.	Stand strong, breathe, and project more—practice using your diaphragm to project.
Eye Contact	We can see your eyes at different points of the performance to show you are trying to connect with us—your audience. You can hold eye contact from three angles of the room, so you are showing that you know your content well.	Do a few more practice rounds before presenting to a live audience.
Expression	The way you say the words and phrases shows you are interpreting the mood and content to communicate to the audience. You may change expressions in different parts as the mood shifts or ideas become more serious or light-hearted.	Practice in the mirror and record yourself so you can see your facial expressions and body language, which generates interest in the topic.
Pace	You stay within the time allowed. You perform with a pace that matches the content and mood; it is slow enough for us to hear and process the words and fast enough for us to feel the rhythm. You may slow down to emphasize certain parts or let an important idea really resonate with the audience.	Time yourself with a friend so you can get a sense of the pacing; maybe add or cut something if needed.
Pronunciation	You clearly practiced and know the words you've written, especially technical ones. The audience is not distracted by phrasing or unclear pronunciation.	Look up words in the dictionary only to listen to pronunciations; practice saying them; write phonetic pronunciation on your notes.
Professionalism	You clearly prepared for the performance. You stand strong (no swaying), say "thank you" at the end to signal closure, stay for a moment to accept the applause, and your demeanor treat the topic and audience with respect.	Not yet—eye contact, clarity and projection of voice, tone, and pace make the presentation difficult to follow.

After all the performances were loaded, we hosted a listening day. All the students brought earbuds to class, and they listened and wrote notes to their peers across the six classes I taught. Because they were recorded, we could listen multiple times, too. Listeners wrote comments to their peers digitally so they could all see the impact of their writing on others. Perhaps some would write a poetic response or add a third perspective to the two-voice poem.

How Permanent Is the Artifact? To What Degree Is It Identifiable?

The reason we chose to share the audio files on our school website and with first names only was because the voices and first names are identifiable and shared as part of the school technology platform. Students didn't want screenshots of their performance being shared in other social media places, and the audio file seemed less risky of any violation of that. The school's Google Site was not searchable and was permanent as long as I was a teacher at the school.

Notes about Google permanence and access:

- When a Gmail address is closed, access and availability to Sites are also closed.
- The Google Doc is a collaborative written poem that lives on both Google Drives for the students and me as a teacher in the learning management system.
- The video recording of students exists in each of their Google drives for their self-assessment.
- The notes students write to their peers on paper have the first names of the students and a specific comment that students were directed to tape/stick in their notebooks.
- The audio recording is a digital genre/medium of the written two-voice poem. This file lives on the Google Site and was deleted from my phone Voice app.
- The digital comments students write to each other live on the Google Site.

Learn the Poem Form: Two-Voiced Spoken Word

My entry point into the e-Poetry Framework began with the text and performance form of spoken word (Weinstein, 2018; Williams, 2015). Spoken word can trace its roots back to civilizations where storytelling, chants, and poetry were passed down orally from generation to generation. These oral traditions were often performed in various social and cultural settings, serving as a means of entertainment, education, and cultural preservation. Greek and Roman poetry was often performed orally at public gatherings, festivals, and competitions. In the 19th and 20th centuries, spoken word continued to evolve with movements such as the Beat Generation of the 1950s (Ginsberg, 1956) and the Black Arts Movement of the 1960s (Baraka, 1969) playing significant roles. These movements emphasized spoken word as a means of social and political expression, often performed in intimate settings such as coffee houses and clubs. Slam Poetry emerged in the late 20th century as artists like Gil Scott-Heron and The Last Poets infused their poetry with elements of music and rhythm (Eleveld, 2005). The rise of competitions in the 1980s and 1990s introduced a competitive performance-oriented aspect to spoken word, with poets competing in poetry slams to showcase their talents and express their views on social issues (Bishop, 2019; Smith & Kraynak, 2009).

The first National Poetry Slam was held in 1990. Louder Than a Bomb (LTAB) is the largest youth poetry festival (Coval, 2010; Young Chicago Authors, n.d.). Started in 2001 in Chicago, over 500 youth perform solo and group poems in a tournament-style competition. LTAB is now Rooted & Radical Youth Poetry Festival and is in 13 states because of the writing, performing, and community it cultivates as a dedicated space to the voice of young people. In the 21st century, contemporary spoken word poetry continues to thrive in various forms and mediums. From YouTube to live performances in theaters and spoken word cafes, poets from diverse backgrounds and all ages use their voices to address topics such as identity, inequality, and activism, connecting audiences on a personal and emotional level. The digital files of spoken word can go viral, spreading ideas to change hearts and minds.

Spoken word is meant to be performed; so, what it looks like on the page is not as important as how it sounds and how the speaker performs it. In other words, it is not a poem in that the stanzas and line breaks that communicate meaning are not visible to the listener. Still, there is writing involved. The spoken word artists write multiple drafts of the poem and even continue to change it with subsequent performances. In fact, no two performances are identical, and the poem is forever dynamic.

This unit will introduce you to several spoken word poems, but if you'd like to stop here and watch/listen to a few, here are some suggestions to easily search on YouTube. Most of these were performed on Def Poetry, Button Poetry, and even TED stages: Sarah Kay (n.d.), "Hands"; Elizabeth Acevedo (n.d.), "Hair"; Rudy Francisco (n.d.), "Rifle"; Carlos Andrés Gómez (n.d.), "Where are you really from?; Mahogany L. Brown (n.d.), "Black Girl Magic"; William Nu'utupu Giles (n.d.), "Captain America."

Study Mentor Texts

We began with spoken word pieces using the rhetorical triangle as a way of analyzing the text and the speaker. Students drew a triangle in their notebooks to capture details of ethos, pathos, and logos. I modeled and taught each part as we watched Marshall Davis Jones' "Touchscreen" (2011). Marshall Davis Jones is a spoken word artist known for his powerful and thought-provoking performances. One of his notable pieces is "Touchscreen," which critiques society's over-reliance on technology and the disconnect it can create between people. He explores the digital age, focusing on the ways touchscreen devices like smartphones and tablets have changed the way we interact with one another and the world around us.

In the poem, Jones describes how our lives have become increasingly mediated by screens, with people constantly glued to their devices, scrolling through social media feeds, and engaging in virtual communication. He highlights the irony of being more connected than ever before while simultaneously feeling more isolated and disconnected from each other. He argues that technology creates barriers between people and inhibits genuine human connection.

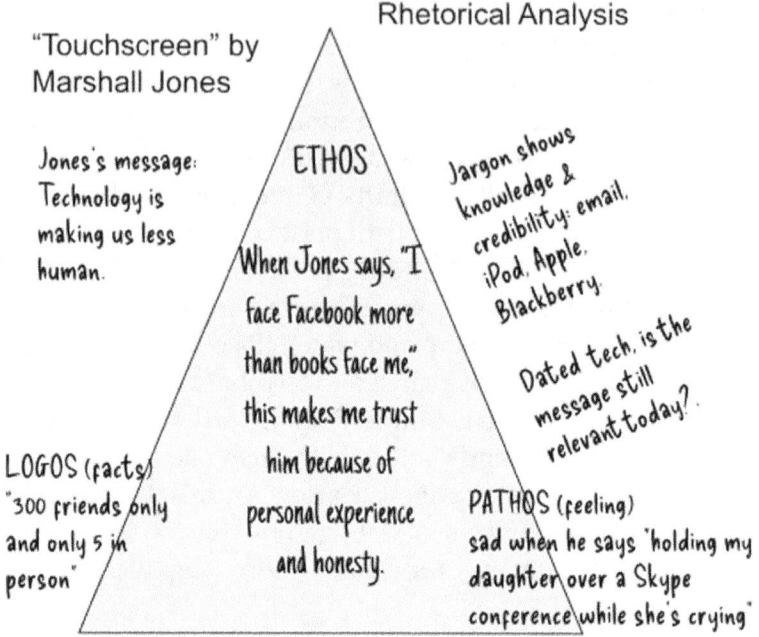

FIGURE 8.2 "Touchscreen" rhetorical triangle analysis

First, students write down their thoughts on the affordances and limits of technology on relationships, forming their own ideas. Then, students listen without the gestures. Then, they watch with Jones' gestures. I invite them to share with a partner what fact was most compelling and what phrase hit their hearts the most. And then, they revisit their notebook to add what Jones had to say about this issue of digital connections.

Next, I hand out a printed version of the spoken word piece so that we can do the rhetorical analysis. Students paste the printed version on one side and draw a triangle on the other side (see Figure 8.2 for an example). I walk them through the rhetorical triangle of ethos, pathos, logos, and ways the speaker establishes this with both written words, expression of words, and gestures:

Ethos:

- When he says, "I face Facebook more than books face me," this makes us trust him because he is relating to us (as his audience).

- Jargon: email, iPod, Apple, Blackberry—This shows knowledge of technology but also that it is dated.

Logos:

- When he says, "3000 friends online…5 in real life," those factual numbers are compelling.

Pathos:

- When he says, "I'm holding my daughter over a Skype conference while she's crying." it hits my heart and shows the contrast between virtual and physical contact.

After studying Jones' spoken word text and performance, I invited students to synthesize their responses in a blog post. At the time, we used Kidblog (now FanSchool). Students logged into the classroom account and used their paper notebook reflections and triangles to type their analysis. Students did this because I wanted them to see how this short text is doing a lot of sophisticated argumentative work from experience but also with technical terms and facts and to prepare them to write their own.

Student A: *Marshall explores the social issue of technology. He says it makes us less human and I mostly agree with him. He says, "Doubled over, we used to sit in treetops til we swung down and stood upright, then someone slipped a disk, and now we are doubled over at desktops." This is strong, but I do not agree with him on this statement. I believe that nature and being outside are still something kids with all forms of technology do. I spent days in the Summer outside from 12:00 to 8:00 playing basketball with my friends. This is something that will never be lost in humans. However, I agree when he says, "I update my status…to prove I am still breathing." This is true for some people. Just being on Facebook, Instagram, or Snapchat is a way that they want people to realize that they exist and they still are here. That is another issue that should be talked about. The influence of social media is the real problem in most cases.*

Student B: *This poem gives me very mixed emotions. While I believe that technology has a very big part in today's society and some people rely on it for everything. I still don't believe the issue has become crucial. It will be a big problem later, but right now, I believe that I am still human, and I don't always sit "doubled over at desktops." So, the world is relying more on technology than before, but is that really a bad thing? We can interact with family from across states. We can get information that can save lives. We can live longer! Most importantly I think technology itself is improving the human race. Medicine, Security, Money managing. All of these things are the backbone of our entire life, and technology is improving them. So maybe it isn't that bad after all. Marshall did do a great job on this poem and it does make myself think if I rely on technology as much as he says. He is making the issue talked about.*

The genre study is a very important first step in this digital poetry project. I have modeled the process of studying one spoken word piece. We also studied a partner poem that showed two different perspectives to help students start thinking about how two voices can express the complexities of an issue, with various stakeholders having space to voice their experiences. We studied "Hir," a poem about transgender youth by Alysia Harris and Aysha El Shamayleh (2010) (see Figure 8.3). We also studied "Counting Graves" by The Steinmenauts (2013), which is about gun violence.

We read the texts. We listened to the voices performing the words. We watched the performances. Students knew that these texts were powerful on the page, but the embodied voices mattered even more. And as we moved from the single-voiced pieces to the two-voiced pieces, students realized that the additional voices impacted the message. This rhetorical strategy evoked empathy in the speaker, which the audience felt, and in considering points of view, the speaker showed attention to the different experiences and implications of the issue.

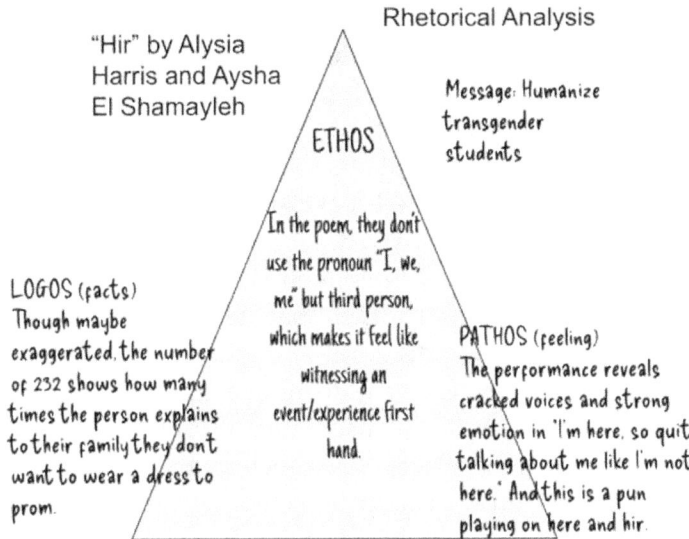

FIGURE 8.3 "Hir" rhetorical triangle analysis

Gathering Topics, Partnering, and Drafting

The next step was for students to select a current event issue of concern to them—animal rights, health, body image, restorative justice, immigration, environment, marriage equality, refugees—and write a two-voiced poem.

To begin, students partnered up to do a rhetorical analysis of a news article. We used articles from *NewsELA*, an online education site our school had purchased a license for, but this has some free access options, too. Students repeated the rhetorical analysis process with news articles, e.g., identifying the jargon and logos used in that article.

Then, students collaborated to create a two-voiced poem using the jargon and logos but to do so in the voice of stakeholders in the issue. By considering the points of view of those affected by the issue, students exposed points of view as a method to convey the dimensions of the issue and evoke pathos in the audience. Capturing how different stakeholders would use the jargon and logos illuminates the complexity of the issue and evokes pathos (and hopefully consciousness).

For example, two students read a news article about how environmental groups advocate for sustainable agricultural practices that reduce the use of genetically modified organisms (GMOs). Students learned about the importance of preserving milkweed and other native plants to ensure the survival of monarch butterflies. They crafted a two-voice poem from the perspective of a CEO and an activist.

To present the poems in spoken word style, we practiced reading a lot. Students and their partners spent a lot of time exploring the pacing, rhythm, and time. They rewatched "Hir" and "Counting Graves" to notice the way people step up to voice their parts. We used this VEEPPP (Volume, Eye Contact, Expression, Pace, Pronunciation, Professionalism) self-assessment rubric to help us celebrate our strengths and set goals for development. Table 8.2 is a general presentation rubric you can use for a number of activities; eye contact, however, is not necessary in an audio recording, so students do not have to memorize the two-voiced poem, though it should be well-rehearsed.

Finally, we held a performance day where students performed their multi-voiced pieces (see Figure 8.4). To offer another example of the various topics of interest to students, three seventh-grade students (pseudonyms) read an article from *NewsELA* about polar bears in zoos. They began with a brief introduction: "In this piece, we are talking about how zoos are hurting polar bears. And people are wondering and deciding whether it is best to return polar bears to their native environment, but, due to global warming, nobody is sure what to do because polar bears may not have enough space to live there." They selected three perspectives on the issue to capture in this poem: A polar bear floating on a block of ice further and further away from its home, a zoo employee, and a young zoo visitor (Table 8.3).

Then, they began reading their poem together while we recorded it. The entire presentation took under 90 seconds

Other topics included the following: "Zookeepers Using Dogs," "Marriage Rights: Waiting in Line," "Surfer Girls in

FIGURE 8.4 The open mic area of Sarah's classroom. Photograph by author

Bangladesh," "Syrian Refugees in the US," and "From "Alien" to Noncitizen."

The audience-classmates took notes on a "Listening Sheet" (see Table 8.4) on the jargon that showed ethos in the speaker, the logos that were most convincing, and the pathos or the aspects of the piece that most appealed to their hearts.

TABLE 8.3 Student Poem: Bear, Employee, Visitor

Polar Bear	Zoo Employee	Zoo Visitor
Home is only 60 thousand miles away. Stuck in this space away from my life without a trace.	A little cage, a prison, a cell that holds all polar bears captive in between feedings, that's where I work.	I come to see the animals disappointed they won't come out to play. I go inside to find adorable winter white fir, wondering if they miss home.
I am drifting further from home on this ice cap.	I can move among animals' homes in minutes.	My feet are hurting; I want to go home.

TABLE 8.4 Listening Sheet: Student Example

Partners/ Topic	What I know before Listening	Jargon	New Facts	New Insights and Questions
Polar Bears in Zoos / Eve and Jennifer	I enjoy seeing Polar Bears at zoos.	Ice cap Captive	Polar bears are losing their native home due to climate change	Zookeepers are a voice, but are they part of the problem, or are they saving Polar Bears?
Alex and Sam / Chemicals	Butterflies I see in my backyard.	GMOs Milkweed Monarch	GMOs impact the milkweed, which impacts the Monarch population	The companies are trying to feed the masses with affordable food, but are we willing to pay more for cereal if sustainable practices cost more?

Learn the Tech

When making digital recordings and engaging with websites on Chromebooks, several ISTE (International Society for Technology in Education, 2024) student standards can apply, particularly those related to digital creation, collaboration, and digital citizenship. Here are some relevant ISTE (2024) Student Standards:

1. Empowered Learner (Standard 1): Students leverage technology to take an active role in choosing, achieving, and demonstrating competency in their learning goals. This can apply to students using Chromebooks to self-assess and showcase their learning.
2. Digital Citizen (Standard 2): Students recognize the rights, responsibilities, and opportunities of living, learning, and working in an interconnected digital world. Contributing content to websites involves understanding concepts like digital privacy, security, and ethical use of information.
3. Knowledge Constructor (Standard 3): Students critically curate information from digital resources (*NewsELA*), construct knowledge (Two-Voice Spoken Word Poems),

and express themselves creatively using various digital media (audio recording).
4. Creative Communicator (Standard 6): Students communicate clearly and express themselves creatively for a variety of purposes using the platforms, tools, styles, formats, and digital media appropriate to their goals. Contributing to websites allows students to express themselves creatively and effectively through multimedia content. and
5. Global Collaborator (Standard 7): Students use digital tools to broaden their perspectives and enrich their learning by collaborating with others and working effectively in teams locally in preparation for more global engagement if the site were public and the teacher collaborated with schools in other countries.

Collaborative website creation can involve students working together to design, develop, and publish content. Most Chromebooks come with a built-in camera app. You can access it by clicking on the launcher (bottom left corner) and searching for "Camera." Once the camera app is open, you can switch between photo and video mode.

Recording the Audio-Video as Self-Assessment
When practicing the performances and for the actual performance, learners used the video feature in their Chromebooks to record themselves for self-assessment as they developed their public speaking skills.

- ♦ Select video mode. There are several online tools and apps available that allow you to record videos directly from your Chromebook's camera. Some popular options include Screencastify, WeVideo, and Clipchamp. These tools usually require you to install a Chrome extension or app from the Chrome Web Store.
- ♦ After installation, follow the instructions provided by the tool to start recording. Click the record button to start recording.

- Click it again to stop. Before recording any videos in a school setting, make sure to check with your school's policies regarding video recording and privacy. Some schools may have specific guidelines or restrictions in place.
- Once you've recorded your video, make sure to save it in a secure location. You can save it to your Chromebook's local storage or upload it to cloud storage services like Google Drive or Dropbox. If you need to share the video with others, ensure that you follow appropriate protocols for sharing sensitive or educational content in a school environment.

Audio Recording for Publication

There are several voice recording apps available for Chromebooks. You can find them on the Chrome Web Store by searching for "voice recorder" or "audio recorder." Some popular options include "Audio Recorder" and "Voice Recorder & Audio Editor." Once you've chosen the app you want to use, click on it to open its Chrome Web Store page. Click on the "Add to Chrome" button to install the app. Follow the prompts to complete the installation. Begin your conversation with the Chromebook's microphone positioned appropriately to capture both your voice and the voices of others involved in the conversation. Ensure that everyone involved is aware that after stopping the recording, the app will typically prompt you to save the recording. Choose a location to save the recording, such as your Chromebook's local storage or cloud storage services like Google Drive. Some apps may also allow you to edit the recording or add tags/comments for organization purposes.

Now, you can share the audio files with students in other classes. You may have this feature on your learning management system, such as Google Classroom, but if you want to use Google Sites, you can upload the audio files. If you have 15 partners in six classes, like I did, this will take a little bit of time to upload (Figure 8.5).

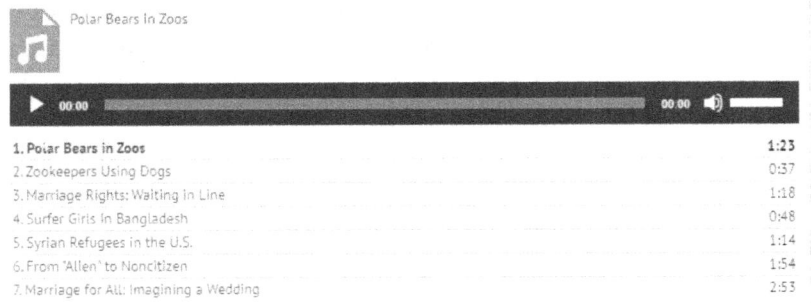

FIGURE 8.5 Example of recorded spoken word playlist

Publication

Now that you have your downloaded sound bites, navigate to the specific page where you want to add the audio file or create a new page to publish.

1. Once you're on the desired page, click on the "Edit" button or the pencil icon to enter edit mode.
2. Click on the place on the page where you want to insert the audio file.
3. In the toolbar at the right side of the page, click on "Insert" (the plus icon).
4. Choose "Audio": From the dropdown menu that appears, select "Audio."
5. Upload the Audio File: A window will pop up, allowing you to upload the audio file from your computer. Click on "Choose audio" or "Select audio file from Drive," depending on where your audio file is located. Navigate to the location of the audio file on your computer or in your Google Drive, select it, and click "Open" or "Select" to upload it.
6. After uploading the audio file, you may have the option to adjust settings such as autoplay, loop, and controls display. These options may vary depending on the version of Google Sites you are using.

7. Once you have uploaded the audio file and adjusted any settings, click on the "Save" button to save your changes. After saving your changes, you can preview how the audio file will appear on your Google Site.
8. If everything looks good, click on the "Publish" button to make your changes live on your site.

Interaction and Celebration

To promote and document interaction with the content, remember to consider privacy, moderation, and community guidelines when implementing commenting systems on your Google Site to ensure a positive and safe user experience. Google Sites does not natively support commenting directly on the site itself. However, there are workarounds you can implement to enable commenting functionality. Embed a Google Form onto your Google Site, allowing visitors to fill out the form and submit their comments, questions, or feedback. Alternatively, students can write comments on sticky notes, and you can create a paper envelope for people to deliver their notes to peers in other classes. See Complimenting Writers in Chapter 4 (Table 4.3).

For assessment, use the rubric and artist statement we've offered throughout the book (see Table A8.1 in Appendix for further processing and rubric). You will want to look especially at the collaboration element in this assessment and encourage students to consider the impact of co-creating a poem and audio recording with a partner. What did they learn about this process? What did they learn about themselves? What did they learn about their partner? We encourage you to debrief this whole class as the focus of this chapter is this co-creation. Focus on ways the co-creators helped one another do their best, shine, and contribute to the project—in the poetry, the voicing of the poetry, and the technology piece. Take time to surface this.

Depending on your school grading policies, this project and others in this book lend themselves to standards-based grading rather than a single grade for the entire process: 1) Reading and literary analysis; 2) Brainstorming; 3) Drafting; 4) Revising: 5) Speaking; 6) Listening; 7) Multimodal presentation. Each one of these can be assessed and included in the gradebook along the way as evidence of the writing process if needed.

Reflection

In exploring two-voiced spoken word poetry, it's crucial to remember that the form is flexible, allowing students to speak in their own rhythm without strict adherence to meter or rhyme. The mentor texts we study provide a wealth of strategies for employing ethos, pathos, and logos, encouraging students to voice their ideas powerfully and authentically. This approach not only teaches rhetoric through contemporary art but also connects these lessons to current events, helping students understand and engage with the world around them.

The nature of spoken word as an embodied performance was a highlight for students, though recording performances, especially on sensitive topics, raised privacy concerns. Using audio recordings instead of video ensures students' safety by preventing the sharing of images on social media and addressing privacy issues while still allowing students to express their passions for social justice. This balance is essential for fostering a safe, inclusive learning environment.

Educators who incorporate the e-Poetry Framework center students' voices and empower students to make decisions about their performances (e.g., identifiability) and topics (e.g., environmental issues, animal rights). By guiding students to use technology responsibly and creatively, we help them become effective digital citizens and communicators. This chapter underscores the importance of respecting students' autonomy while harnessing the power of spoken word poetry to inspire and educate through collaboration among peers who create and learn from one another's content creation.

Reference List

Acevedo, E. (n.d.). *Hair*. Retrieved August 18, 2024, from https://www.elizabethacevedo.com

Baraka, A. (1969). *Black magic: Sabotage, target study, black art; collected poetry, 1961–1967*. Bobbs-Merrill.

Bishop, D. (2019). *The creation of poets: How poetry slam effects literacy development and identity in young writers*. University of Massachusetts Lowell.

Brown, M. L. (n.d.). *Black girl magic*. Retrieved August 18, 2024, from https://www.mahoganylbrown.com

Coval, K. (2010). Louder than a bomb. In J. A. Sandlin, B. D. Schultz, & J. Burdick (Eds.), *Handbook of public pedagogy: Education and learning beyond schooling* (p. 395). Routledge.

Eleveld, M. (2005). *The spoken word revolution: Slam, hip hop & the poetry of a new generation*. Sourcebooks, Inc.

Francisco, R. (n.d.). *Rifle*. Retrieved August 18, 2024, from https://www.rudyfrancisco.com

Giles, W. N. (n.d.). *Captain America*. Retrieved August 18, 2024, from https://www.williamgiles.com

Ginsberg, A. (1956). *Howl and other poems*. City Lights Publishers.

Gómez, C. A. (n.d.). *Where are you really from?* Retrieved August 18, 2024, from https://www.carlosandresgomez.com

Harris, A., & El Shamayleh, A. (2010, November 4). *Hir* [Video]. YouTube. https://www.youtube.com/watch?v=IRLSgPQG0c4

International Society for Technology in Education. (2024). *ISTE student standards*. ISTE. Retrieved August 18, 2024, from https://iste.org/standards/students

Jones, M. D. (2011, October 12). *Touchscreen* [Video]. SpeakeasyNYC. https://www.youtube.com/watch?v=video_id

Kay, S. (n.d.). *Hands*. Retrieved August 18, 2024, from https://www.sarahkay.com

Smith, M., & Kraynak, J. (2009). *Take the mic: The art of performance poetry, slam, and the spoken word*. Sourcebooks, Inc.

The Steinmenauts. (2013, April 23). *Counting graves* [Video]. YouTube. https://www.youtube.com/watch?v=1dgt2dBqazw&t=39s

Weinstein, S. (2018). *The room is on fire: The history, pedagogy, and practice of youth spoken word poetry*. SUNY Press

Williams, W. R. (2015). Every voice matters: Spoken word poetry in and outside of school. *English Journal, 104*(4), 77–82.

Young Chicago Authors. (n.d.). *Louder than a bomb*. Young Chicago Authors. Retrieved August 18, 2024, from https://youngchicagoauthors.org/archive/louder-than-a-bomb

Appendix

TABLE A8.1 Rubric: Recorded Two-Voice Poem

	Recorded Two-Voice Poem Rubric and Artist Statement
Assignment Component	*Meet Expectations (2 pts)*
Final e-Poetry Submission	You submitted a complete, polished poetry artifact. In this final piece, you considered peer and facilitator feedback and carefully edited the piece for form, style, grammar, language, technology, etc.
Poetry Craft Moves Standard: Write arguments to support claims in an analysis of substantive topics or texts using valid reasoning and relevant and sufficient evidence.	Two-Voice Poem • Content comes from a news report, evidence of notes, and a citation (logos) • Two voices—where they are separate and where they converge—are clear or signified in some way (font, color, columns) • The selected voices represent key perspectives on the news topic (ethos) • Use pathos in respectful ways (e.g. not spectacle or appropriation)
Technology Component Standard: Use technology, including the Internet, to produce and publish writing and to interact and collaborate with others. https://iste.org/standards/students	Audio Recording • Effective use of volume: louder or softer for certain phrases to emphasize ideas; volume does not distract from the message • Expression of words and phrases is intentional is related to tone (feelings of the voice) and mood (seriousness of the topic) • Pace matches the content and mood; slow enough that listeners can hear every word but not too slow as to miss the key meaning • Pronunciation shows evidence of rehearsal and care in learning the jargon and key names in the poem. The listener is not distracted by unclear phrasing • Professionalism: The published recording is the best version with a clear title, reading, and stop • File .MP3
1 Revision Strategy	The final piece and/or artist statement demonstrates that at least one revision strategy from the course was attempted. (A writer may choose not to use a revision, but trying it out is an important part of the process.)

(Continued)

TABLE A8.1 (*Continued*)

Recorded Two-Voice Poem Rubric and Artist Statement	
Assignment Component	*Meet Expectations (2 pts)*
Artist Statement	Your artist statement discusses your **co-creation process,** identifies the craft moves and revision strategy you implemented, describes a significant aspect of your writing process or experience, and describes what you learned as a creator from this process.

Scoring Scale:
Meets Expectations (2 pts): Thoughtfully completed in a way that reflects course lessons and meets criteria.
Partially Developed (1): The product is only partially developed, or it reflects course lessons in a limited way. Revisit course activities and lessons or instructor feedback for further development.
Missing/Incomplete (0): The assignment is missing or incomplete to a degree that it is not able to be scored. Or the artifact does not reflect the assignment guidelines.

Artist Statement (handout offered during class)

- What surprised you about (topic) while you were crafting the project? Give a specific example. (For example... For instance.) What successes resulted from the project?
- Tell us about your process—how did you get from beginning to end in writing this piece?
  - What did you learn about this process? What did you learn about them? What did you learn about your partner? How did you help them shine? How did they help you shine?
- Which mentor texts had the biggest impact on your thinking and writing? (Name the author/colleague, name the text, and explain how you used the mentor texts to inspire your writing.)
- Which craft elements and/or minilessons impacted the revision and meaning of your writing?
- Which peer feedback influenced your choices? Please cite classmates.
- What did you learn about the topic/context/subject of this piece that you may not have known or understood when you first began writing this?
- What do you understand about this mode and genre in particular that you may not have known or understood when you first began?
- What did you learn about yourself as a writer and content creator? (For example. For instance...)

9
Concrete Piles of Positivity with Templates

The visual display of poetry often adds a visceral effect on its audience. We saw that in the haiku GIF and the zip-ode in different ways. When words are placed purposefully in a form (often now through the help of technology), the meaning changes. Our senses are inspired. We can visualize the shapes or concrete poems possibly written on paper for younger poets; we do this to engage them in the writing and meaning, right? How often do shapes inspire us or remind us of certain emotions?

It is almost like a butterfly effect—some shape, place, and experience set off a motion of actions that lead to a different result. I felt this inspiration when I read Kay's (2023) "A Pile of Good Things" poem on social media in response to author Rowell's (2011) words: *So, what if, instead of thinking about solving our whole life, you just think about adding additional good things. One at a time. Just let your pile of good things grow.* Kay (2023) built upon reading a work of literature and then pulled out a meaningful quote to create a pile poem inspired by good things. The pile provides a discernable build-up through her words in the essence of Smith (2023), who explains that life and poetry are built upon choices. We, as educators, are always making small choices, adding in minute shifts that flutter into new outcomes for our learners.

Not only is a pile poem representing a pile of good things, it is sparked by words of another, making it cyclical in meaning and demonstrating the flow of inspiration we all get and yet sometimes cannot put into words. I was inspired to utilize the positivity and visual representation of this form through digital means.

Plan with the e-Poetry Framework: Pile Poem Template

What Is the Learning Purpose?

I (Stefani) was inspired to create a prompt for others to write about positive life experiences—small or big—and pile them up into one poem (Figure 9.1). The idea of the template was sparked by incorporating a digital tool the poet can quickly create and share. An educational template is a support tool (often for scaffolding) with a guided format, language, or style to make learning and application more streamlined. A template often limits the time it takes to learn a new strategy or tool and focuses primarily on content learning.

The pile poem activity was led by teacher choice and textbook-driven. The teacher's choice comes from the connection between the concrete poetry form inspired by any text-based quote. In addition to my interest in the pile form, I thought about how often we have students choose quotes from text to summarize, reflect, or connect to. I also wanted this to be a visual, concrete submission, so I was further inspired to consider how to utilize Canva templates for this visual form (more on that below). Although I put the content first, I am also thinking in the back of my head about how technology can further enhance the application. Templates allow for accessibility for creators of all ages. The joy of sharing these "good" piles in quick, easy digital PNGs was very intriguing. I want learners to see how they can create a visual form to represent the meaning, use a digital template to enhance their work and purposefully engage with the technology to collectively create multiple piles of good things. And don't we need more good to go viral?

Concrete Piles of Positivity with Templates ♦ 177

e-Poetry Framework
PILE POEM

Digital

Purpose & Choice
Teacher choice and textbook driven. Building a visual pile poem connected to text quotes.

Mode & Choice
Mixed: Informational-poetic structure with a list base; potential for narrative and storytelling if it is a character, for example.

Audience: Private to Public & Choice
The audience is the World Wide Web; share, what could be a sort of meme/image to tag, share, etc.

Form & Choice
Remix: Concrete pile poem and graphic representation with template support

Nature of Interaction & Choice
Shareable once the template is downloaded, no room for remix on product but the template can be shared for remix.

Permanence & Choice
The student can download the pile poem visual to share. This can be easily edited but would need to be reshared (meaning it is not live).

Genre →

Donovan & Boutcher (2024)

FIGURE 9.1 e-Poetry Framework: Pile poem

What Is the Mode?

The initial intention of a pile poem was meant to be narrative—each line is a fragment of a story, a collection of memories, evidence of experiences—as it shares the stories and experiences of "good things" through this form. We even envision this poem as a brainstorming session for other poems. The pile of good things is not a traditional narrative with a plot, climax, denouement, or resolution. The only thing wrapped up nicely at the end is the e-Poetry creation. However, it can be considered narrative as a collection of auto/biographical scenes and adapted to create piles of information about a topic or even piles of obstacles, character traits, supporting characters, and so on. With the pile enlarging at the bottom, the representation is intended to show the growth of the pile (for good things, that should increase gratitude; yet, if it turns into a negative pile, it could increase stress levels).

What Is the Form?

This is a remixed form of graphic and poetic-a pile poem template for creating a concrete visual. This concrete pile poem provides a poetic shape to communicate a specific message through a graphic form to demonstrate our appreciation of little things. Although the pile poem is not an official form, after Kay's use and our published use of the form on *Ethical ELA* in 2023 (see the piles at https://www.ethicalela.com/pile-poem/), I'd say we can call it a poetic form worth writing with. Also, see Image 9.5 for the Google Search response.

Who Is the Audience?

The use of a teacher-designed template is meant to create a final product that can be shared with peers, school, and beyond. We can celebrate the good things in the world, the positives on a school campus, or the highlights of others. Digital artifacts (e.g., memes, GIFs, shorts) are this generation's language and communication style. We must take advantage of considering how our curricular design can best support learning and digital humanization.

When considering a tool, it is helpful to ask: Does the tool allow for variation in audience? The pile poem can be downloaded as is (i.e., into a JPG) or shared via a link directly to the Canva site. Doing this latter option allows for live updates at any time.

Who Will Interact with the Content? How?

Building upon audience choice, using Canva (not all tools allow for this) easily provides a modifiable nature of interaction if one uses the Canva share link. The student can share the link; even if they edit when someone clicks the link, the updates will show immediately to the audience. However, if they download the pile poem as a JPG, PNG, or PDF, it will be shareable and static. Finally, in consideration of the nature of the interaction, the initial use of the template provides an opportunity for "intended for remix"—this is from the teacher's end, but this models how the students might even create a template for later creations or to share out with a student-designed template.

This can be a great way to spread a message for a public service announcement (PSA) project, a civic-minded commercial, or a campaign assignment in secondary courses. Educators can create a template for conferences, school events, or community events to share and/or promote on social media profiles. There is a lot of potential for use for templates and interaction beyond this chapter as well.

How Permanent Is the Artifact?

Permanence rolls over with the nature of the interaction. With this technology, a teacher might require or allow for options of permanence. I require one permanent download to share with peers for initial feedback. Live links allow for ongoing updates, as noted earlier, and via Canva, comments can be added with modified access to viewers. This is helpful for the feedback and review stages. Building rapport among your learners and guiding them to become responsible and ethical digital communicators will enhance this process (revisit Chapter 2 for ideas).

Note: permanence online might still not be searchable, meaning it might be online if one knows where to find it but wouldn't be linked by name, locations, or through any other algorithm of connection to the school, for example. You and your learners often define this via socials. You might start out with the assumption that everything can be shared socially or go viral due to screenshots, but for the intention of this framework, we presume it to be based on the requirements of the teacher or the choice of the student.

Learn the Poem: Concrete Pile Poem

A pile poem isn't a traditional form, nor does it have many poetic rules other than accumulation or shape (feel free to add your own poetic structures). The concreteness of the pile poem is meant to demonstrate a visual that is metaphoric to convey a building toward an emotional message. Concrete poems have morphed, yes, pun intended, from an abstract art interpretation to the distinct shapes we often associate with them today (Poets.org, n.d.). If the concrete poem was read aloud, the shape would not be clear but the title would guide the tone. The pile represents an accumulation of good things—maybe consider a line for each year of the poet's accumulation (we won't model this, for our age is a private pile of joy). We are focused on good things in this pile, so the visual should represent growth or closure, and it can be positive, lighthearted, deep, or open. The lines are not restricted by syllables or rhyme but should grow in visual length. It can be centered (like a pile of clothes) or justified to the right or left. The idea is to allow this visual form to be splashed in a structure to encourage writing. Below is the first pile poem I wrote:

> *snuggles*
> *from my kids...getting too tall*
> *but always welcome to block my vision*
> *remembering the kindness in humanity through*
> *eye contact, hugs, face-to-face conversations; fresh food,*
> *my dog sitting on my toe; the sunshine in winter, homemade guacamole*
> *peanut butter and chocolate anything; relaxing with my family on*
>   *a Friday night,*

nowhere to go, in my robe; traveling anywhere new; friends reminiscing about old stories
new invites; newborns falling asleep in my arms; ignoring everything else to finish a good book

It is helpful to offer the suggestion of writing a list first before formatting it into the concrete pile. After the list and formatting, the poet might pull out themes of joy or stick with a large variety. As I review mine, I see how much of this pile can be experienced in my robe, so maybe I should've put this into a robe shape—okay, I digress, but my thinking here might be similar to your students' artist statements. Now try it yourself; you might start with a list and then modify it to fit the concrete shape structure. You might invite all your colleagues to do this and bring piles of happiness to your school's community. Imagine the joy of a wall of pile poems in the faculty lounge.

Write Poetically

A pile poem is intended to be a concrete poem about the good things in one's life. The visual form shows growth in words/syllables/line length as you move down. In considering the writing process, the pile could be drafted with more generic elements of appreciation and then grow into subjective, specific elements of good things experienced by the author (see example in Figure 9.2). Start with writing about the self for drafting and examples. Then, this "form" can be used with or without the template for literary characters, historical figures, eras, settings, plots, current events, etc. Once the learners understand the process, they can use it even for summarizing and reviewing.

You can extend the reach of this template and the positivity of its topic to launch a community-wide project. How could you build up your school community or local community by sharing piles and piles of good things? You can send the template with more directions and share the outcomes in a common digital space (e.g., Wakelet, Padlet, Google Site). Use this to celebrate the humans around your community. Think teachers, retirees, staff, unsung heroes, all students. There are many ways to use

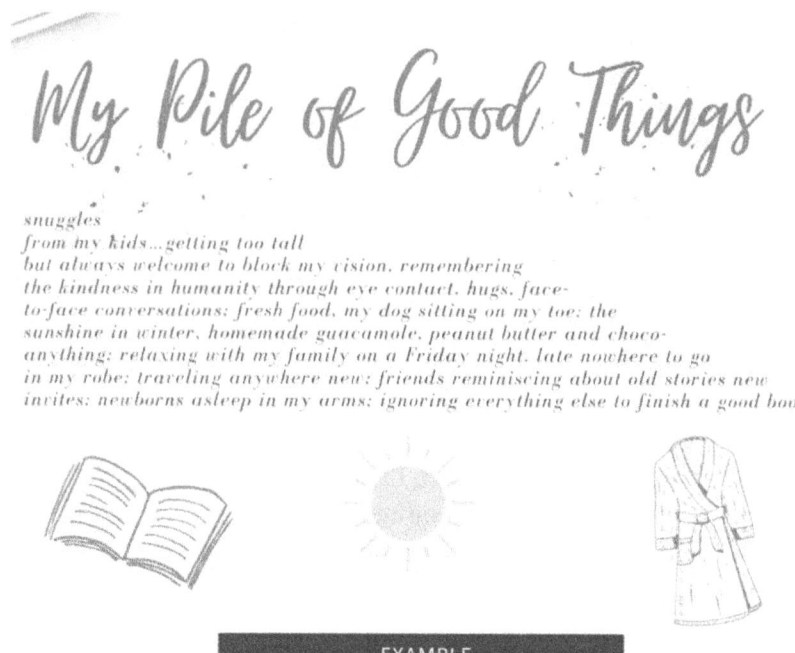

FIGURE 9.2 My pile of good things. Image by author

this mode and form, plus the potential of audience exposure for this type of celebration is unlimited.

Learn the Tech: Teacher-Created Templates

In reference to templates for this chapter, we are speaking directly to you as the designer as an organic design or as a remix to create educator-designed templates. This allows us additional freedom and tailoring for our students' needs. Templates are great scaffolds for learning and igniting creativity (for any age). The allowance of personalizing the template also gives a push to start the process versus solely starting with a blank slate or empty doc (see the end of this chapter for additional pre-made templates for digital poetry).

The tool interface is potentially a challenge and time waster, however, if the intention is to utilize Canva templates for future projects/options, then it is worth the time spent to learn and create the initial template as this process supports Universal Design for Learning (UDL 3.0) (CAST, 2024; return to Box 2.1 in Chapter 2 for more). The use of this template requires learning Canva. Educators, you will need to learn how to create the templates (see below), and students will need to know how to edit, zoom into the font, replace, and possibly add a page (again, see Steps for Template Content Creator section). The example template provides one page of directions, one example page, and one blank template.

Scaffolding this tool allows students to directly add their poems to the template and moves the publication process to provide a choice option in supporting UDL's principle of expression (Skene & Fedko, 2014; Thibodeau, 2024). We are also redefining how we use technology (SAMR framework, see Box 1.1; Puentedura, 2010) to publish and share learners' poems. Again, this allows them to become published poets, and what a good thing that is.

By using a template, the tool is more low-stakes to allow students to test it out, not spend too much time on the technology itself (the learning curve is strongly eliminated) yet provide choices to increase personalization and productive completion rates. You can encourage students to add their own pictures, use https://thenounproject.com/ to find specific images related to their poems, or have them upload drawings.

Canva templates are a great way to use technology with purpose, save time, inspire creativity, and allow for edits along the way. Visual representation in this form is easier to share with audiences as a JPG, PNG, Meme, pic, etc. Students can print out, share, remain anonymous, and be proud of creating and applying a digital representation of their creativity. Providing a template generally limits the time it takes to learn a new tech tool and is also a form of scaffolding. A note about the template: It should still have clear step-by-step instructions on how to use, modify, and personalize the template. As noted previously, a goal of introducing new technology is not to frustrate poets in the process of a learning curve related to technology but to enhance the poem and share it with the world—to bring joy.

Steps for Template Content Creator: Educator

View the copy of this: Pile Poem: Canva Template (https://www.canva.com/design/DAFbIHd0AgM/fWnicX2Yl0xsI209ryBKkQ/view?utm_content=DAFbIHd0AgM) as an initial model and mentor template.

1. Create your free Canva Educator account
2. Design your template (your choice of product): see notes regarding what pages and examples you might add and view the mentor template link. You will also want to edit the directions based on our feedback process, timeline, or other pertinent information
3. Share>More>Template Link (see Figure 9.3)

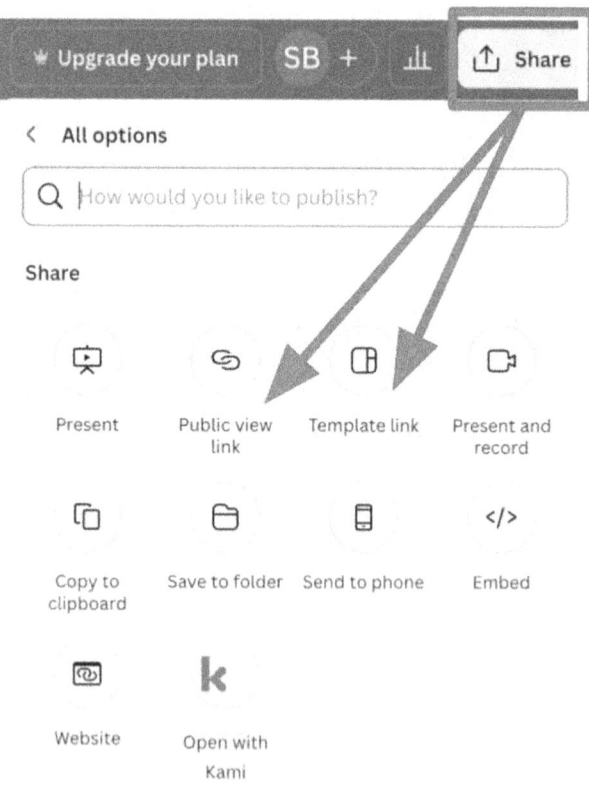

FIGURE 9.3 Canva image example of how to share and publish. Image by author

4. You can share the template link directly with students when ready. You might create a bit.ly to shorten and share in a faster, more accessible way. This is beneficial if you don't have a learning management system (LMS) or other digital community to quickly share the longer template link URL

Tip: If you don't want to use Canva or just want to know how to quickly turn Google Docs into a shareable template, then follow these steps and see the bit.ly access at bit.ly/epoetrytemplate link connected to Figure 3.2 for one template preview example: 1) Go to the Google app (e.g., Doc, Sheets, Drawings) URL; 2) copy the URL and paste where you want to share, delete "edit" after the last "/" slash in the URL; and 3) replace with "template/preview."

Steps for Content Creator: Student (Example)
1. Open the shared template link (when ready during the process of poem-ing) (revisit Figure 9.4)

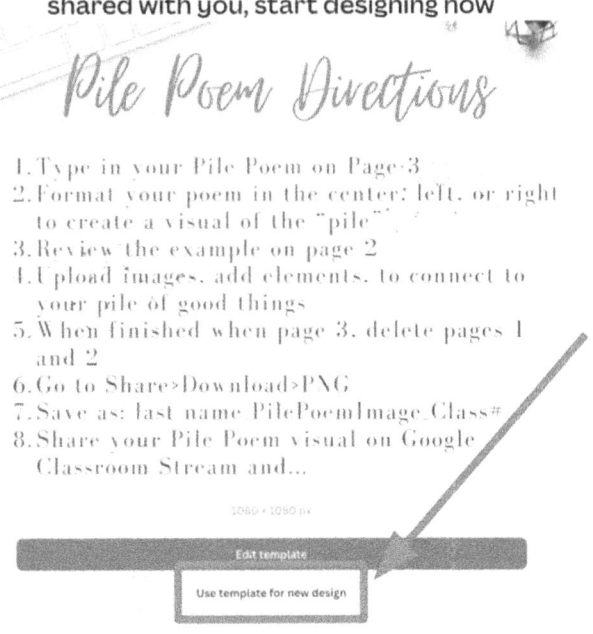

FIGURE 9.4 Example of directions and prompts for using the template. Image by author

FIGURE 9.5 Searching for mentor texts. Image by author

2. Click on "Use template for a new design" (see Figure 9.5)
3. Type in your pile poem on page 3
4. Format your poem in the center, left, or right to create a visual of the "pile"
5. Review the example on page 2
6. Upload images and/or add elements to personalize your pile of good things
7. When finished with page 3, delete pages 1 and 2
8. Go to Share>Download>PNG
9. Save as: last name_PilePoemImage_Class#
10. Share your pile poem visual on Google Classroom Stream or LMS

Study Mentor Texts

As we mentioned, the pile poem is not quite a commonly written poem form—but we trust you will help make it so. Our mentor texts can be found via a general engine search (Figure 9.5), on Ethical ELA (https://www.ethicalela.com/pile-poem/), and in a few other places. We provide a few different examples from educators and elementary students; it is now your time to share our secondary examples.

> hot water cornbread
> sitting next to collards
> on a shiny ceramic plate
> on a drizzly Sunday afternoon
> maybe there will be fried fish or
> chicken wings or perhaps today might
> be a meat-free experimental kind of day
> black eyed peas, brown rice and tomatoes
> also adorn the circular food dish and an ice
> cold glass of sugar sweetened lemonade round
> out the perfect meal. No dessert is needed today.
> (Hurd Wright, 2023)

Teacher-poet Simon (2023) took this into her practice for second-grade elementary students, both the form and mode (see Figure 9.6).

Playing Baseball
When I get a good hit,
I run fast to the bases.
I read a book to my tiger
before I go to sleep. I read by myself.

FIGURE 9.6 Elementary students created pile poems with templates

This is one example of how this can be remixed for one's needs. We can notice or encourage using fonts, colors, sizing, and images to represent tone in the final product.

In addition, for her own practice, Simon (2023) switched the point of view and interpreted this prompt based on her own needs (see Pile of Peeves below). These variations remind us why it's important to have mentor texts and allow poets to process artist statements along the way.

Also, see the end of this chapter for a few more examples and variations of the topic, such as a "Pile of Peeves" (2023) by Margaret Simon.

> Scent of cat pee
> Anxiety at 3 AM
> Morning cafeteria duty
> When I've lost something
> Hitting Send before proofing
> A colleague diagnosed with cancer
> An unconsolable child weeping over a mistake
> The sound of my alarm when I'm actually sleeping
> In carpool line, putting a student back into a toxic environment
> The big white truck with extra tires passing me to make a right turn from the left lane.

Peer Feedback

As mentioned in Chapter 4, we provide various tools to guide your poets through drafting in their writing. The bonus of Canva is that before students download their final PNGs for submission, they can share the link for comments and feedback from peers. You can guide your learners with a feedback protocol (either in Chapter 4 or any other, for example, TAG: Tell, Ask, Give).

1. Click Share
2. Under Collaboration Link, Click>Anyone with the Link
3. Then click>Can Comment
4. Click>Copy link and share it for peer feedback

5. Use the **TAG** protocol: In a comment, **T**ell your peer one way in which you connect with their pile of joy, **A**sk your peer to further expand on one of the good things with a story, and **G**ive your peer specific praise on one element (not simply: Good job!).

Publication

Before your students have downloaded their final product, you will want to decide how they will share this (see Table A9.1 in Appendix for further processing and rubric). Sharing on a public site (whether just with your students or beyond a district access-only site is something to determine beforehand). Allowing your students to learn and also reflect on all the small and big things to appreciate is one outcome of this. You can have students remove names for additional privacy and have them add initials, or since the list of positivity is generally less vulnerable, you might encourage students to add a name to start conversations.

An important note when publishing a PNG or any downloaded creation is to make sure it is shareable. You will want to make sure if students download the poem to their computer, they can easily upload it to the LMS or intended publication platform. Sometimes, this includes an additional step to make the access shareable (e.g., upload the PNG to a Drive and then create a link to share).

As noted above, Canva creations can be shared with live links to allow for real-time edits. Sharing the finished product with this same process also extends the potential of permanence, expands the audience, and allows for the identification of the poet-creator to vary. If you keep the comment allowance after the final creation is shared, you create an interactive e-Poetry setting that can bring further joy in response to the concrete piles but also allows for a quick shift in permanence (e.g., it can be turned off at any time). This option can help with ongoing edits, but caution students not to take this option too literally and make too many edits if this is how you publish.

Reflection

Although the initial intention was to model the template tool, the pile poem continues to be a highlight of my courses. The poem itself has become a moment or "lesson" of pause to remind us of all we are thankful for and how the little things make us happy. When I work with educators, they are also excited to learn that they can be in control of a designed template. Whether it be for this digital poetry lesson or any other multimodal content outcome, having the ability to add some guidance via a template puts more ownership and creativity on both the educator and students.

Templates work well for all ages, social media, the promotion of school activities, or common themes. Adding directions to your templates is always an element of an effective template. I have seen educators use this for many ages and multiple purposes. Using this to share our poetry in digital images is a fun and easy way to start.

Reference List

CAST. (2024). Universal design for learning guidelines version 3.0. https://udlguidelines.cast.org

Hurd Wright, S. (2023). Pile poem. *Ethical ELA*. https://www.ethicalela.com/pile-poem/

Kay, A. (2023). A pile of good things. Twitter/X @amykaypoetry [inactive]. https://www.amykaypoetry.com/

Poets.org. (n.d.). A brief guide to concrete poetry. https://poets.org/text/brief-guide-concrete-poetry

Puentedura, R. (2010). SAMR and TPCK: Intro to advanced practice. http://hippasus.com/resources/sweden2010/SAMR_TPCK_IntroToAdvancedPractice.pdf

Rowell, R. (2011). *Attachments*. Plume.

Simon, M. (2023). My pile of peeves. https://reflectionsontheteche.com/2023/03/24/slice-of-life-challengepoetry-friday-piles-and-trees-of-good-things-and-one-pile-of-peeves/

Skene, A., & Fedko, S. (2014). Instructional scaffolding. *Center for Teaching and Learning: University of Toronto Scarborough*. https://

collegiateteachinginartanddesign.com/wp-content/uploads/ 2018/10/scaffolding-university-of-toronto-learning-center.pdf

Smith, M. (2023). *You could make this place beautiful.* Atria/One Signal.

Thibodeau, T. (2024). What does it mean to scaffold instruction? *Novak Education.* https://www.novakeducation.com/blog/what-does-it-mean-to-scaffold-instruction

Other Pre-made Poetry Templates

https://www.kamiapp.com/library/resources/fuFUpA1GbD5x-diamante-poem-activity

https://floridawriters.blog/using-microsoft-word-to-write-concrete-poetry/

https://www.adobe.com/express/create/poster/poetry

Appendix

TABLE A9.1 Rubric: Pile Poem Rubric

	Pile Poem Rubric and Artist Statement
Assignment Component	*Meet Expectations (2 pts)*
Final e-Poetry Submission	You submitted a complete, polished poetry artifact. In this final piece, you considered peer and facilitator feedback and carefully edited the piece for form, style, grammar, language, technology, etc.
Poetry Craft Moves Standard: Write narratives to develop real or imagined experiences or events using effective technique, well-chosen details, and well-structured event sequences.	Informational-Pile of Good Things poem • Visual represents a pile with longer lengths to each line • Content moves from broad concepts to specifics (in either direction) • Tone is positive and playful
Technology Component Standard: Use technology, including the Internet, to produce and publish writing and to interact and collaborate with others. https://iste.org/standards/students	Shareable PNG from Template • Use the template to share your pile poem • Images, colors, etc., connect to the content • Font and text are easy to read • File is .png or similar (checked for sharing access if needed)

(Continued)

TABLE 9.1 (*Continued*)

Pile Poem Rubric and Artist Statement	
Assignment Component	*Meet Expectations (2 pts)*
1 Revision Strategy	The final piece and/or artist statement demonstrates that at least one revision strategy from the course was attempted. (A writer may choose not to use a revision, but trying it out is an important part of the process.)
Artist Statement	Your artist statement discusses how X informed your written piece, identifies the craft moves and revision strategy you implemented, describes a significant aspect of your writing process or experience, and describes what you learned as a writer from this process.

Scoring Scale:

Meets Expectations (2 pts): Thoughtfully completed in a way that reflects course lessons and meets criteria.

Partially Developed (1): The product is only partially developed or it reflects course lessons in a limited way. Revisit course activities and lessons or instructor feedback for further development.

Missing/Incomplete (0): The assignment is missing or incomplete to the degree that it cannot be scored. Or the artifact does not reflect the assignment guidelines.

Artist Statement

- What surprised you about (topic) while crafting the project? Give a specific example. (For example... For instance) What successes resulted from the project?
- Tell us about your process—how did you get from beginning to end in writing this piece?
- Which mentor texts had the biggest impact on your thinking and writing? (Name the author/colleague, name the text, and explain how you used the mentor texts to inspire your writing.)
- Which peer feedback influenced your choices? Please cite classmates.
- What did you learn about the topic/context/subject of this piece that you may not have known or understood when you first began writing this?
- What do you understand about this mode and genre in particular that you may not have known or understood when you first began?
- What did you learn about yourself as a writer or content creator? (For example...For instance...)

10

Playing with Words: Enhancing Poetry Through Gamification

"Gamified"
Blink, blur, breathe
Check my stats
Noise-canceling gear, couch
Viewing, Trolling
Next level, Easter eggs
> *Blink, blur, breathe*
> *Whistle blows, stampede*
> *Hundreds of fans, bench*
> *Cheering, crowding*
> *End zone, goal, net*

Bask in glory
Stepping out, ready, set, play
Setting up, 3, 2, 1…face off
Explode, my senses activate
Finger muscles, eye muscles, anxiety
The sweat of emotion, not pain
Gasses my flow, my addiction
Bitcoins, credit galvanize a flame that traps me
In the alternate world, Twitch.tv
> *Bask in glory*
> *Stepping out, ready, set, start*
> *Step, run, 3, 2, 1…game on*
> *Explode, my senses activate*
> *My heart tugs at all my muscles, anxiety*
> *The sweat of pain, not emotion*
> *Gasses my flow, my addiction*
> *Standings, scores galvanize a flame that traps me*
> *In the anaerobic world, ESPN.go*

> Beg for the physical, not the digital
> Addicting mirror, my reflection gazing, staring, cannot look away
> Must run, yet the magnetic noises of the circuit pull me back
> Multi-platform, streamer, no longer a noob
> No longer rekt, I will be a Legend of this game
>> Beg for a digital break, not the challenge
>> Addicting endorphin release, pushing my body to the limits
>> Must run, yet the needed interval break distracts me
>> Remix the right reps, just go, no longer an amateur
>> No longer destroyed, I will be the MVP of this game
>>> (Boutelier, 2021)

How do you define "game?" I (Stefani) have asked this many times when teaching and researching gamification. The answers vary along with responses to the question: What is your favorite game? This second question usually encounters ideas that stretch our thinking to demonstrate how varied we define games as sporting events, board games, logic games, and video games cover the broad areas involving our experiences in a game. Games are part of everyday life (yes, some have responded with the game of life), yet competition runs between self, others, and nobody. It's not always about winning. It is often more about the challenge, the critical thinking, the training, the collaboration, and the community involved in the process. After all, the Olympics were meant to result in camaraderie and peace as a social construct and not necessarily end with an ultimate champion.

Why not have fun when teaching and learning? This chapter considers how gamifying curriculum increases engagement and retention (Dicheva et al., 2015; Lee & Hammer, 2011). When we consider digital poetry, we consider the creation and not solely the evaluation of poetics as a critical skill. This chapter will do both: It will explore the alignment of gamified pedagogy to increase engagement in both writing, learning, and critiquing poetry.

We want to continue to push you to innovate in ways with the e-Poetry Framework in mind and with multi-varied mediums. This chapter won't focus on one poem but will explore how we can use a gamified curricular lens to further enhance digital poetry in our design. Let's explore the difference between gamification and game-based pedagogy (Box 10.1).

> **Box 10.1**
>
> Game-based = active learning within a game framework or intrinsically game theory (e.g., role play, strict competition) vs. Gamification = game elements in instructional design (e.g., badges, gameboards) (UWCTE, 2024; Wright, n.d.)

Gamification (Writing Process)

Game theory, game-based pedagogies, and a game-based model are all the same frameworks that might guide your entire year and live a game-like setting in your classroom. For this chapter's exploration, we focus and expand on the use of gamification for designing, scaffolding, and retaining elements of digital poetry as a strategy and not a framework.

Gamification is the application of game-like mechanics (e.g., competition, points, check-ins) to non-game entities (e.g., content learning) to encourage increased engagement and application (Dicheva et al., 2015; Teachthought, n.d.). Gamification turns a learning unit or lesson into a game for the completion of a task (e.g., goal, writing activity, creation) as a design mechanism (Boutelier, 2024; Dicheva et al., 2015; Keene, 2022; Smiderle et al., 2020). McTighe & Willis (2019) provide a short and guided process to consider how gamification can align with your instructional design process:

1. Establishing a desirable goal
2. Offering an achievable challenge
3. Providing constant assessment with specific feedback
4. Acknowledging progress and achievement en route to a final goal (p. 16)

Step 3 is a key element in considering the humanizing and growth element of any design mechanism. All previous chapters return to the importance of workshopping and the benefits of feedback from others. There is an end goal, possibly competition, and/or both internal and external motivation. The process of gamifying may be viewed differently depending on the age of the learners you work with, the content, or even the general context (e.g., time of year, day, current events). We can all find community in games; even adults I work with realize their engagement when something is gamified and to the point. As noted in many chapters, gamification is another UDL 3.0 support for designing and supporting the agency of all learners (CAST, 2024).

Although there is a crossover between gamification and game-based curriculum, the key for this chapter is to consider how we might gamify with digital tools to engage learners with poetry. We will provide a variety of ways you might gamify the craft of digital poetry. We might consider designing a gameboard (see Figure 10.1) to help organize the writing and workshopping process (refer to Chapter 4). Your gameboard can simply lead students through your e-Poetry Framework writing and publishing process, or you can amplify the gameboard and provide choices, obstacles, and additional tasks (think of Monopoly and see Figure 10.1). You might also use gamification to provide mentor text options to analyze in a fun and structured process on a digital gameboard.

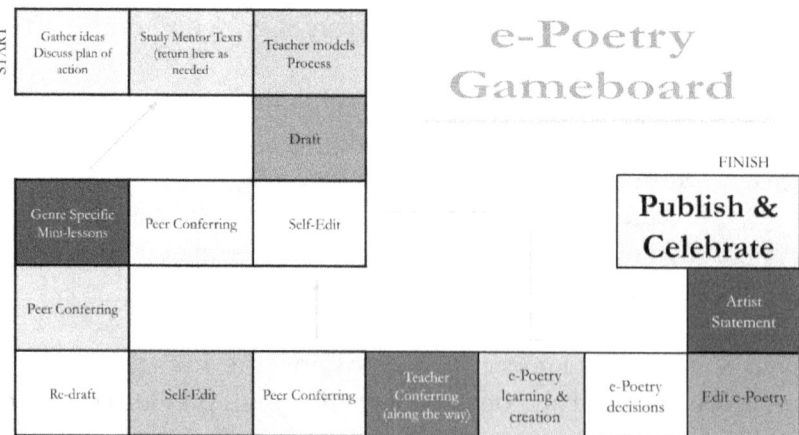

FIGURE 10.1 e-Poetry gameboard for students. Image by Author

Gamification (Tools)

This chapter's concept of gamification might be a review, or maybe it is entirely new, but consider: How are you already gamifying your curriculum? Do you use badges? Quests? Or Choose Your Own Adventures (CYOA)? You might even design with hyperdocs, project-based assessments, or full units that you've gamified in a way. Using brackets, often popularized in connection to tournaments, is another way to gamify the learning process to increase motivation for the task. We all use elements of gamification in our design through many of the free and readily available ed tech tools. Think about how often you might use some of these for formative assessment: Kahoot, Gimkit, PearDeck, Quizziz, and Nearpod. Or the original gamified slide deck (does anyone remember when we only had PowerPoint?) with Jeopardy. These examples all provide gamified elements to consider for poetry writing, poetic device practice, or verse analysis.

One example for an entire poetry unit might be built around a poetry March Madness game (see Figure 10.2 example and think about using it during April's poetry month; also see Table 10.1). The poetry unit is gamified to engage learners to read, rate, and evaluate poetry along the way toward a "winner." Learners

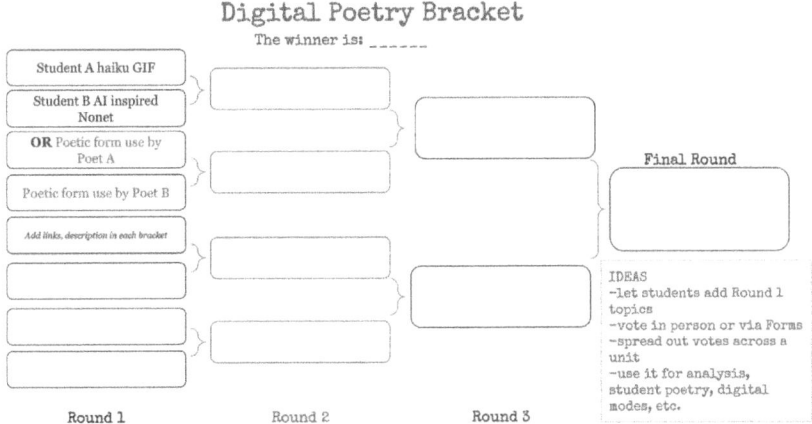

FIGURE 10.2 Digital poetry bracket. Image by author

TABLE 10.1 e-Poetry Gamified Ideas

Gamified Strategy	Digital Poetry Support
Badging or Micro-credentials	**Badge Tracker** to show poetry writing throughout the year (e.g., badge for haiku, badge for slam poem)
	Flippity offers a free tool: https://www.flippity.net/
Gameboards and Brackets	See Figures 10.1–10.3
	There are plenty of gameboard templates online; use Sheets, slides, Canva to design. Use it as a process or include more choice options (think Monopoly—e.g., land here and write a haiku)
	https://www.mudandinkteaching.org/news/poetrymarchmadness
	Flippity offers Bracket templates
Poetry Escapes, Quests, or Scavenger Hunts	BreakoutEDU had a poetry month-themed offering
	Digital poetry Escape (paid): https://teachnouvelle.com/product/poetry-review-activity-escape-room/
	https://sites.google.com/site/7thpoetryreview/
	Virtual Breakout to create a poetry escape room
	Partner Scavenger poem (think Found poem with rules)
	Digital **scavenger hunt** to analyze and explore various poems in connection to a larger theme, in connection to a longer text, or in connection with expository writing
	https://thekingdomandthekeys.weebly.com/poet---path.html
	Place-based: https://medium.com/fielddaylab/kids-in-verona-wisconsin-use-siftr-to-write-poetry-b8e14fa6f147
Choiceboards, Tic Tac Toe Board, or Hyperdocs	**Click and Drag** (manipulatives) a found poem in connection to a text in Flippity.
	https://theteachingfactor.wordpress.com/2016/02/19/5-ideas-for-blending-gamification-in-your-ela-classroom/
Collaborative poems	Create with cloud-based tools (e.g., Google Docs) through game boards. This might be rolling dice/numbers to pull out prompts. This might seem similar to Mad Libs
	Random Name Picker can be filled with topics, themes, and poetic devices to include in a fun and short poetry writing game in Flippity
	Randomizer to include various forms, modes, and topics for a fun poetry writing challenge after learning and practicing various types (Flippity)

(Continued)

TABLE 10.1 *(Continued)*

Gamified Strategy	Digital Poetry Support
Common gamification ideas for ELA	Formative assessment quizzes: Gimkit, Quizizz, Kahoot, Zoom Polls
	Interactive and synchronous platforms: Peardeck, Nearpod
	https://www.pinterest.com/velagicl/gamification-in-the-ela-classroom-middle-school/
Digital **Metaphor Dice**	https://rollthedice.online/en/roll/metaphor-dice-roll

develop a rating system and rate the poems, and a winner (poem/poet) emerges at the end of the unit. See a few ideas in the templated bracket in Figure 10.2 and access the QR code in Figure 10.3 to create your own. There are also plenty of bracket templates online for free (e.g., Flippity, Figma, Kami). Students can fill in round one with their favorite mentor texts, and you can mix in music lyrics, student poetry, forms, etc.

Earning badges or micro-credentials (e.g., complete mini-tasks such as publishing poems) leading to a digital poet certification (teacher-created challenge) is another way to align with gamification. This could interplay with the gameboard idea as well. Students might earn a badge (or simply a point) based on

FIGURE 10.3 Digital bracket template QR code. Image by author

form, mode, presentation slams, peer feedback, e-Poetry meme creator, or other topics. A tic tac toe board for a poetry unit adds UDL-enhanced design of action and expression through choice (CAST, 2024). Plenty of free software and programs are readily available to provide templates for badge collection to create leaderboards, board games, and matching games to support fun play with poem-ing online. Table 10.1 curates some ideas from this chapter, plus additional gamified e-Poetry strategies for your consideration.

Gamifying the e-Poetry Framework

In case you haven't noticed, we love the possibilities of digital tools as supplements to support content creation through poetry. Often, having both options (i.e., digital and hands-on) lends a hand to more inclusion, hybrid learning, or possible last-minute curricular changes. I have a set of Metaphor Dice (i.e., three dice that act as a writing tool prompt and ignite writers to think creatively in metaphoric ways) that I share with my adult learners (see Figure 10.4). Teachers can grab a free set from https://www.metaphordice.com/product/teacher-recipient/ or use https://rollthedice.online/en/roll/metaphor-dice-roll. We first discuss why metaphors are important in the learning process, why we should use them to teach, and why we would turn it into a poetry

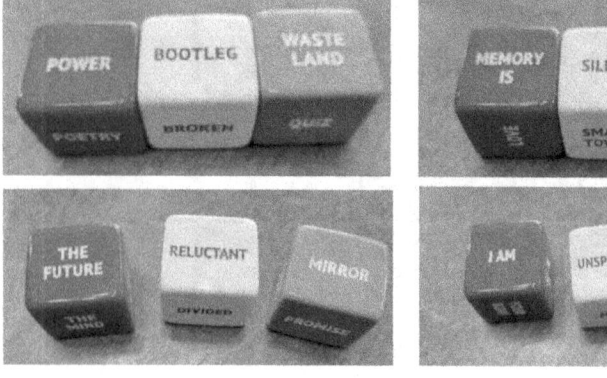

FIGURE 10.4 Rolled Metaphor Dice examples. Image by author

lesson. The idea of metaphors can extend beyond poetry to help support multiliteracies, engage students in ownership, and make connections across content (think about the mathematical possibilities).

Although our sharing of gamification might fit into many variations of your use of the e-Poetry Framework, we will provide a condensed narrative of the framework's cyclical questions to possibly duplicate. We will roll the dice for this modified e-Poetry example with Metaphor Dice.

What Is the Learning Purpose?
This could be a remix of student-centered engagement and PLC to include gamification.

Using Metaphor Dice in person or the digital version provides a plethora of combinations. The metaphors are built upon a triad of concepts, adjectives, and objects. It is suggested that the rolled metaphor be followed up with "which is to say" to expand on the figurative meaning in a poetic text further.

What Is the Mode?
The mode of the Metaphor Dice could vary and be a remix based on your needs and the content you are using. You can start by having everyone write with the same three words rolled with actual dice or the online version. The role of three words fits into a combination from this list: Concept-adjective-object (https://www.metaphordice.com/new-page/; e.g., the past, reluctant, animal; or my heart, well worn, candle). You can first invite learners to do some personal writing to apply those words to their lives and then make it more biographical by writing about a character or a thought leader in your conceptual unit (e.g., women's rights activists and Indigenous writers).

What Is the Form?
The form for playing and poem-ing with Metaphor Dice is what I would call a structured-free verse—yes, we are playing with words here. You provide the keywords and comparison, but the poet can add as many lines, syllables, and devices as they want.

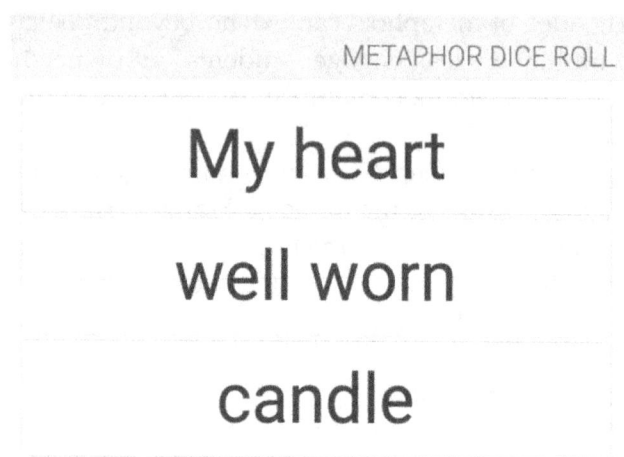

FIGURE 10.5 Online Metaphor Dice example from random word selector. Image by author

You might spice up the game with some challenges, such as adding rhyme, imagery, or personification (Figure 10.5).
Stefani's outcome:

my heart is a well worn candle
which is to say
this bleeding alter
a flame throbbing hope
Pound, beat, flicker
a wick transplanting feelings of
past fireworks, darkness
fluttering light
igniting a spark of experience
pound, beat, flicker
to escort my body's hearth

Who Is the Audience?

Can the audience here be the poet? Can the gamification of writing with metaphors be meant to excite the writer? Yes, of course it can. Learners are inspired by writing, discovering, and sharing metaphor poems in safe digital spaces with peers, so the audience engages in the game. Extending the audience is up to you and the students. You may include Metaphor Dice in other e-Poetry activities (e.g., a mini-lesson or revision strategy) or exchange the haiku for a metaphor poem, for example. You can also determine who will interact with the content and how **permanent** the poem is.

If we were to take the metaphor poem and convert it to a GIF, use a template, create a video short, or share it via any other mode, then the e-Poetry creation would become more permanent and interactive.

Reflection

Games can bring forth a variety of emotions and can be interpreted in many ways, as described in the opening poem and throughout this chapter. Sometimes, the sweat of competition, the stress of timers, or the play of words brings purpose and extension to our learning environments—the growth through feeling uncomfortable. We, as educators, often don't need a reason to increase community in our classroom. Many of us already gamify intentionally or because some of these "gamified" practices unintentionally (or not) support effective pedagogical practices (e.g., collaboration, choice, scaffolding). If this wasn't already part of your intention, it is important to know why and how you might gamify any digital poetry process. Whether you are the MVP or on the sidelines, you have the skills to gamify poetry to add excitement, intrigue, and a bit of laughter into your practice.

Reference List

Boutelier, S. (2021). Gamified. In S. Donovan (Ed.), *Rhyme and Rhythm: An anthology of high school sports poems*. Archer Publications.

Boutelier, S. (2024). Gamified ungrading: Playing with andragogy and feminist instructional design. *Feminist Pedagogy*, 4(4), Article 7. https://digitalcommons.calpoly.edu/feministpedagogy/vol4/iss4/7

CAST. (2024). *Universal design for learning guidelines version 3.0.* https://udlguidelines.cast.org

Dicheva, D., Dichev, C., Agre, G., & Angelova, G. (2015). Gamification in education: A systematic mapping study. *Journal of Educational Technology & Society, 18*(3), 75–88.

Lee, J. & Hammer, J. (2011). Gamification in education: What, how, why bother? *Academic Exchange Quarterly, 15.* 1–5.

Keene, B. (2022). *Game-based learning and the ISTE standards. Becky Keene: Educator-Author-Changemaker.* https://beckykeene.com/2022/07/20/game-based-learning-and-the-iste-standards/

McTighe, J., & Willis, J. (2019). *Upgrade your teaching: Understanding by design meets neuroscience.* ASCD.

Smiderle, R., Rigo, S.J., Marques, L.B., Coelho, J. A., & Jaques, P. A. (2020). The impact of gamification on students' learning, engagement and behavior based on their personality traits. *Smart Learning Environments, 7*(3). https://doi.org/10.1186/s40561-019-0098-x

TeachThought. (n.d.) 10 Strategies to make learning like a game. https://www.teachthought.com/learning/make-learning-like-a-game/

UWCTE University of Waterloo Center for Teaching and Excellence. (2024). Gamification and Game-based learning. https://uwaterloo.ca/centre-for-teaching-excellence/catalogs/tip-sheets/gamification-and-game-based-learning

Wright, C. (n.d.) Game-based learning vs. gamification: What's the difference? https://blog.mindresearch.org/blog/game-based-learning-vs-gamification

Epilogue: Embracing the e-Poetry Journey

Dear Teachers,

As we conclude this journey of e-Poetry, we invite you to reflect with us on the transformative experiences and insights gained through this journey. *Teaching Poetry in a Digital World: Inspiring Poetry Writing through Technology in Grades 6–12* has offered a comprehensive framework for integrating poetry and technology in your classrooms. Now, we turn our attention to the impacts and discoveries you've made. Perhaps there were tensions and problem-solving, but there was creating and learning. We anticipate there has been a lot of poetry from students and that you have a few of your own to share. Maybe you contributed your pile poem to the class collection or recorded a two-voiced spoken word poem with a colleague. You are a poet. That's right. A poet. Okay, an e-Poet. We'd like to invite you to come over to www.ethicalela.com to continue your poetic journey by writing with us during our monthly Open Write for educators and during our National Poetry Month celebration, Verselove, when we try to write a poem a day.

    But before you leave this page to join us online, let's reflect. What have you learned about genre, the writing process, and technology? What have you learned about your community? How have you gotten to know faculty, staff, families, community, and, of course, your students at different levels? How have you connected with other schools? What has changed as a result of the poetry shared beyond the physical space of school and into the digital spaces? Do your students see themselves as changemakers because of their two-voiced poems? Have they connected with artists in their school because of the Hallway Haiku-GIF? Have you guided your learners to use AI in their journey ethically? How big is your pile of good things now? Okay, so those were a lot of questions at once, but look at all you've learned.

And what about the students? We imagine you have seen learners who were once labeled as non-writers or were maybe resistant to poetry, even school, because of past negative experiences with writing. Are students more confident in their writing process? Have students learned about what poetry can do in the realm of digital spaces and how to expand their knowledge of how genre works?

We hope you and your students have embraced genre as the heart of content creation. The genre is the situation you, the teacher, your students, and PLC have created with the e-Poetry Framework. Purpose, mode, form, audience, interaction, and permanence drive content and create genre. Our goal has been to stir understanding of genre with repeated e-Poetry creations. We hope that you are ready to try some new genres; the options are endless as there are hundreds of poetic forms and technology tools to experiment with. In our physical, embodied spaces and the digital spaces that are intangible or difficult to see or grasp, we can take note of the affordances and limitations of each poetic form and tool for the audience—always putting the human complement first.

Looking Back at Our Journey

Let us look back at what we uncovered in our book. We highlight key elements and leave you with questions to further ponder the digital poetry we explored. In Chapter 2, we began with the evolving concept of literacy, emphasizing digital, visual, and AI literacies. Through this lens, you've explored how technology can foster creativity and critical thinking while ensuring that pedagogical goals and ethical considerations remain at the forefront. How have you integrated these evolving literacies into your teaching? What new understanding have you gained about the intersection of digital tools and equitable, inclusive teaching practices?

Chapter 3 focused on the power of choice in e-Poetry composition, highlighting the importance of both student and teacher decisions in shaping the learning experience. How has the framework for authentic e-Poetry composition influenced your approach to fostering student agency and engagement? In what ways have your choices about purpose, mode, form, audience, interactivity, and permanence impacted your students' learning and ethical considerations?

In Chapter 4, we examined writing process approaches to poetry and technology, emphasizing collaboration and practical steps for creating a dynamic classroom environment. How have you applied these strategies to your teaching practice? What role have mentor texts and active participation played in shaping your students' engagement with writing, revising, and publishing poetry?

Chapter 5 introduced the concept of haiku GIFs as a means to celebrate the school community. How has this approach enriched your students' connection to their school environment? In what ways have you seen the creative process of turning haikus into GIFs enhance literary and digital skills while fostering school culture?

Exploring place-based poetry in Chapter 6, we looked at zip-odes and YouTube Shorts to connect students with global and historical contexts. How have these strategies impacted your students' understanding of the relationship between place and people? What reflections have emerged from their digital creations?

Chapter 7's exploration of AI and poetry with the nonet form questioned the role of AI in poetic creation. What insights have you gained about the intersection of artificial intelligence and human creativity? How have you approached using AI to support the poem-ing process in your classroom?

In Chapter 8, we examined the rhetorical strategies of spoken word poetry and the transformation of news stories into two-voiced activist recordings. How have these techniques enhanced your students' ability to use rhetoric for advocacy and highlight overlooked perspectives? How has technology played a role in sharing their work?

Chapter 9 discussed the creation of pile poems and the use of digital templates like Canva to enhance visual and emotional impact. How have these tools and templates facilitated student engagement and creativity in your classroom? What pedagogical benefits have you observed from using such digital resources?

Finally, Chapter 10 explored gamification in poetry for writing, analyzing, and increasing engagement. How have you applied these concepts to increase engagement in digital poetry? What playful yet purposeful approaches have you found effective in enhancing your students' interaction with poetry?

Looking Forward

As you reflect on these chapters and your experiences, consider how genre is at the heart of the writing composition process. The e-Poetry Framework was designed to create a genre that encapsulates the essence of digital and poetic creation, engaging you and your students in meaningful ways. Perhaps you're inspired to experiment with new genres and digital tools, knowing that the possibilities are endless. Remember, the e-Poetry Framework is a guide, not a constraint. It invites ongoing exploration and innovation.

Our call to action is to remain attentive to both the analog and digital spaces we inhabit. Notice the affordances and limitations of each poetic form and technological tool and recognize that it's perfectly acceptable for the audience to be themselves. Personal engagement can be as impactful as any public performance.

As you continue to inspire and engage your students, we hope you carry forward the insights and experiences from this book. Embrace the endless possibilities, keep experimenting, and let your creativity guide you. The realm of e-Poetry is vast, and your role as educators is vital in shaping how these elements intersect and evolve.

With gratitude and excitement for the journey ahead,
Stefani and Sarah

Index

Note: Page numbers in **bold** and *italics* refer to table and figures, respectively.

accessibility innovation 7
access to resources 39
Acevedo, E. 159
active learning 195
ADHD, poems about 128, 132, *133–135*, 134–135, 138
AI *see* artificial intelligence
AI literacy 18, 125
AI + Nonet 12, 124–126, *127*, **149–150**; AI poem generator 144–146; artifact 130; audience 128–129; content, interaction with 129–130; content creation 138–140; critiquing 138–140; e-Poetry Framework 126–130, *127*, 140; form 128; learning purpose 126; mentor texts 138–140; mode 126–128; nonet poem 130–131; poem analysis 141–142; poem generator 142–144; technology 131–138
AI poem platforms 140–141; *see also* poem analysis
AI Poetry Tools **141**; *see also* poetry
algorithms 9
American Privacy Act of 2024 28
Angello, A. 21
animation 59, 88
"app" language 21
Archie, K. 101
argumentative essay 41
argumentative mode of learning 40–41
argumentative writing unit 152
Armenian Genocide 104–107, 110, 118
Art 10
artificial intelligence (AI) 9, 30–31
artificial poetic intelligence 124
artistic forms of creation 18
ASCII (American Standard Code for Information Interchange) 22
audience 45–47, 53

audience's attention and trust 152; artifact 157; audience 154–155; audio recording for publication 168; content, interaction with 155–157; e-Poetry Framework 152; gathering topics, partnering, and drafting 163–166; interaction and celebration 170–171; learning purpose 152–154; mentor text 159–163; mode 154; poetic form 154; recording the audio-video as self-assessment 167–168; technology 166–167; two-voiced spoken word 158–159
audio 99
audio recording 43, 157
authentic e-Poetry composition 11
"The Autumn of the Patriarch" (Marquez) 44
Azerbaijan's ethnic cleansing 106

Baiocchi, Regina Harris 78
Beat Generation 152
"Black Girl Magic" (Brown) 159
Borges, J. L. 44
Boutelier, S. 3, 21, 30, 124, 125, 132, 193–194
Brown, M. L. 159

Canva 13, 31, 110, 114–118, 183; GIF in 88–89; templates 176, 183
"Captain America" (Giles) 159
Cazden, C. 22
"Cell artwork by 113" *83*
Chaotic Loudness GIF QR Code *91*
ChatGPT 130, 132
ChatGPT3.5a *133*
ChatGPT3.5b *133*
ChatGPT4 134
ChatGPT4o 17, 137
child sexual exploitation 28

The Circuit (Jimenez) 44
"Circuits" (Anna) 44–45
closed media group 47
Co-Learn with AI *139*
collaborative classroom environment 11
collaborative e-Poetry 22
collaborative Google doc 154
collaborative whiteboard 40
complimenting writers **65**
composing poetry 5–6
cookie-stealing/sharing settings 28
COPPA student privacy laws 27, 31
Cortazar, J. 44
"Counting Graves" (Steinmenauts) 162
COVID-19 28
Creative Communicator 167
creative literacy 18
creative self-expression 5
critical literacy 18
critical pedagogy 95–96
Crovitz, D. 18
cyberbully 28
cyber poetry 9

Daley, M. 100
Dalton, B. 22–23
degree of interaction 36
device variation 9
Devitt, A. J. 67
digital artifacts 178
digital bracket template QR code *199*
Digital Citizen 166
digital citizenry for content creators 7, 16–17, 23–26; artificial intelligence 30–31; consume and produce texts 20–21; digital privacy and safety 26–27; digital reflection 31–32; equity 28–29; legal and ethical considerations 27–28; literacies 18; multi-digital art forms 22–23; privacy risks in digital poetry projects 29; technologies 18–20; technologies and their associated literacies 21–22
Digital Citizenship 10
digital communication 45
digital content 7
digital creators 7
digital critiquers 7

digital equity 28
digital exploration 21
digital humanization 178
digital interactions 17
digital literacies 9–10, 13, 17–18, 22
digital media 10, 21, 25, 31, 167
digital platforms 9, 11
digital poetry 7–9, 19, 21–22, 95; with active interaction 22; with passive interaction 22; reflexive practice 21
digital poetry bracket *197*
digital realm of content creation 36
digital recordings 166
digital shadow 27
digital shorts 12, 96, 98; decision-making table **111**
digital story 27
digital texts 18; descriptors 23; temporary art 21; types 22
digital writing 9; text-based 20
Dirk, K. 86
di Rosario, G. 8, 22
Donovan, S. 3, 21, 58
draft & re-draft 59

educational tech (ed tech) 10
educational template 176
ELA *see* English language arts
Elbow, P. 60
electronic multimedia texts 9
El Shamayleh, A. 162
Empowered Learner 166
English language arts (ELA) 10; standards 56; teacher 86; and technology 4
English Language Development (ELD) 10
e-Poetry 37; intended for remix 48; interaction 48; modifiable content 48; shareable 48; static 47–48; understanding 125; units 51
e-Poetry Framework 8–11, 22, 28, 36–37, *38*, 58, 68; AI + Nonet 126–130, *127*; artifact 50–51; audience 45–47; content, interaction with 47–49; decisions 64; feedback 37; form 41–45; Haiku GIF *75*; learning purpose 37–40; lesson 8; mode 40–41; place-based poetry 96; reflection 51–53; student's expressed need or hope 39; teacher, role 39; template **52**; Zip-ode Shorts 97

e-Poetry game-board for students *196*
e-Poetry Gamified Ideas **198–199**
Eppink, J. 87
Esquinca, B. 44
Ethical ELA 58; writers 128
ethical publication practices 29–30
example phrases **65**

faceless shorts 99–100
faceless social media campaign 99–100
facilitate asset-focused peer conferring 60
Family Educational Rights and Privacy Act (FERPA) 27, 31
Federal Trade Commission (FTC) 27
Figma 40
flash poetry 22
forced exodus 106
form **66**
formative assessment 39
four-part blog series 74
Francisco, R. 159
Fuentes, C. 44

GAI *see* generative artificial intelligence
game-based curriculum 196
game-based learning 13
game-based model 195
game theory 195
gamification 13
gamification, enhancing poetry through 193–196; audience 202–203; e-Poetry Framework 200–201; form 201–202; learning purpose 201; mode 201; tools 197–200; writing process 195–196
"Gamified" (Boutelier) 193–194
gamified pedagogy 194
gamifying digital poetry 13
Garrison, D. 40
generative artificial intelligence (GAI) 124–125
generative e-Poetry 22
genetically modified organisms (GMOs) 164
genocide 107
genocide education 96, 98, 104
genre 64–68, **66**
genre-specific mini-lesson 63
"Get in the Halloween Spirit with 8 Bone-Chilling Stories" (Sanin, Cortazar, Quiroga, Fuentes, Borges, Esquinca, and Rulfo) 44
GIF (Graphics Interchange Format) 17, 39, 59, 85–90
GIF QR Code *91*
Giles, W. N. 159
Gimkit 197
Global Collaborator 167
global web 47
Gómez, A. 159
Google Doc 40, 47, 85
Google symbols 59
GPT 125; *see also* ChatGPT
GPT4o 132
Grabill, J. T. 9
Graham, S. 56
graphic forms of digital content 43

haiku 43, 73–74; artifact 76–77; audience 76; content creation, steps for 88–90; content creators 76; e-Poetry Framework 74–77, *75*; form 74–76; hallway haiku 77–85; hallway haiku observation table **80–81**; learning purpose 74; mode 74; parts 78; publication 90–91; shifting to GIF 85–87; structure of 79; study mentor texts 88
Haiku Anthology, The (Van Den Heuvel) 78
haiku GIFs 12, 58–59, **62–63**, **93–94**, 175
"Hair" (Acevedo) 159
Hallway Haiku GIFs 74–76
"Hands" (Kay) 159
Harris, A. 162
Hayles, K. 22
Hicks, T. 9
"Hir" rhetorical triangle analysis 162, *163*
historical poems 6
Holocaust education 96; Guidance **105**
human-centered digital citizenry 17
humanizing element of digital poetry 37
human-to-tech explorations 9
hybrid literary 42
hypermedia 9

identifiability of content 51
Ignatow, D. 42
imagining reading and writing 20

infographics 18
informational essay 41
informational mode of learning 40–41
Instagram 47, 96, 99
instruction **65**
interactive e-Poetry setting 189
International Society for Technology in Education (ISTE) standards 7, 10, 18–19
interpreting 18

Jimenez, F. 44
Jones, M. D. 159
Joy, S. L. 102
JustYA 42, 58

K–12 curriculum 4
Kahoot 197
Kajder, S. 20
Kay, S. 159, 175
Kids Online Health and Safety Report 27
kigo 78
Kinnell, G. 40
Knowledge Constructor 166

large language models (LLM) 125
Latinx literature course 44
learning management systems (LMS) 45, 88, 130
liberated haiku 78
LICEcap 90
literacy 11
literacy standards 18
looping 88
"Lost" (Joy) 102
Louder Than a Bomb (LTAB) 158
Lowell, A. 42

machine poetry 9
Magic School 130
making literature 18
Mann, C. 102, 113–114
Marquez, G. G. 44
Martin, J. 114
math literacy 18
McTighe, J. 195
medium **66**
memes 18, 39
Mercado, N. 40
messaging 88
Metaphor Dice *200*, 200–201

metaphorical thinking 5
Miami, O. 100
Miller, C. R. 68
mirror-point-wonder (M-P-W) conference 60
mode **66**
mode-based writing 43
moral digital citizenship 17
Morgenthau, H. 107
Mullen, H. 42
multi-digital art forms 22–23
multimedia 22
multimedia standards 10
multimodal audiences 8
multimodal literacies 22
Multimodal Literacies Standard Across Grade Levels **19**
multiple forms of digital content 43–45
music lyrics 6

Nagorno Karabagh (Artsakh) 106
Naji, J. 4
naming writing by modes 65
narrative mode of learning 40–41
National Council of Teachers of English (NCTE) 11, 17
National Poetry Slam 158
"Navigating Genres" (Dirk) 86
Nearpod 197
neurodivergence 128
Nonet Ode to ADHD 138; *see also* ADHD, poems about
nonet poems 43, 130–131; *see also* AI + Nonet
non-game entities 195
Norris, D. 102

Oklahoma's Multimodal Literacies Standard 7 18
online harassment 28
online media creations 17
OpenAI 140; *see also* ChatGPT
Open Education Resource 58
open social media 47
Ottoman Empire 104, 106
Output (AI Poem Generator) 142–144

pacing guides 39
Palco, J. 125
paragraph form 41
participatory media 20
PearDeck 197

pedagogy 18–19
peers 46; conferring 60; conferring protocol **61**
permanence 50–51
personal data 26
pile 43
"A Pile of Good Things" (Kay) 175
"Pile of Peeves" (Simon) 188
pile poem 175–176; artifact 179–180; audience 178–179; concrete pile poem 180–181; content, interaction with 179; content creator, steps form 185; e-Poetry Framework 176, *177*; form 178; learning purpose 176; mentor texts 187–188; mode 178; peer feedback 188–189; rubric **191–192**; teacher-created templates 182–184; template content creator, steps form 184–185; write poetically 181
place-based poetry 95–96; artifact 99–100; audience 98; content, interaction with 99; content background 104–109; e-Poetry Framework 96; learning purpose 96; mentor texts 102–104; mode 98; poem and tech with content 113–117; poem form 100–102; poetic form 98; YouTube Short 109–112; zip-ode poem 98–118; Zip-ode Shorts *97*
plagiarism 58
PLC *see* professional learning community
Plumly, S. 40
podcasts 18
poem analysis 141–142; prompt 142
poem generator 142–144
poeming with AI, question-response **129**
poetic forms of digital content 43
poetic structure 5
poetry 4–6; communicative forms 3–4; composing 5–6; and machine learning 125; opportunities for students to engage with 5–6; overview 3; reading 124
private notebooks 46
Proctor, C. P. 22–23
professional learning community (PLC) 40, 152
project-based learning 36
prose form of digital content 41–42

prose poetry 42
Publication Party 64
public platforms 46
public service announcement (PSA) project 179

QR code *113*
Quiroga, H. 44
Quizziz 197

reactionary GIF 87
reading assessment 39
reading poetry 6
recorded two-voice poem **173–174**
redefinition (SAMR) 125
reels (Instagram) 99
remixing 18
rhyming scheme 131
"Rifle" (Francisco) 159
Rowell, R. 175
rules 9
Rulfo, J. 44

Sandmel, K. 56
Sanin, C. 44
SchoolAI 130
school policies 39
Scott-Heron, G. 158
screenshots 130
searchability of content 50
self-harm 28
self/human post 17
short digital video format 96
Shorts (YouTube) 17; permanence of 99
Shovan, L 42
Simon, M. 188
Slam Poetry 158
Smith, M. 175
social justice slam poems 6
social media 50, 86, 98–99; followers 98
spoken word recordings 152; artifact 157; audience 154–155; audio recording for publication 168; content, interaction with 155–157; e-Poetry Framework 152, *153*; gathering topics, partnering, and drafting 163–166; interaction and celebration 170–171; learning purpose 152–154; mentor text 159–163; mode 154; poetic form 154; recording the audio-video

as self-assessment 167–168; technology 166–167; two-voiced spoken word 158–159
"Still Water" 101
student-poets-GIF makers 76
student privacy 27
student's social media audience 98–99
studying mentor texts 58
substitution, augmentation, modification, redefinition (SAMR) model 7–8
supplementary learning 40
syllables 77, *138*, 180
symbolism 5
Szymborska, W. 40

teachers 46
teacher's role in writing process 57
technologies 7–8, 11; associated literacies 21–22; consume and produce texts 20–21
techno poetry 9
template 99
temporary nature of content 50
text 88
textbook-driven curriculum 39
text structure **66**
third-party/machine distribution 17
tic tac toe board 200
TikTok 96, 109
"Touchscreen" rhetorical triangle analysis 159, *160*
Turing Test 125, 131
TV broadcasts 92
two-voiced spoken word 154
two-voices 43

UDL (Universal Design for Learning) 20
UDL 3.0 183, 196
United States Holocaust Memorial Museum 107
Urban Haiku (Baiocchi) 78

Van Den Heuvel, C. 78
VEEPPP (Volume, Eye Contact, Expression, Pace, Pronunciation, Professionalism) self-assessment 155, **156**, 164
"A Very Old Man with Enormous Wings" (Marquez) 44
video recording of students 157
visual e-Poetry 22
visual literacy 18
visual media 87
vocabulary 5

WCAG (Web Content Accessibility Guidelines) 20
Web 2.0 interfaces 20
"Where are you really from?" (Gómez) 159
"Where is Mansfield, TX?" (Norris) 102
wi-fi networks 110
Willis, J. 195
Worldclass Instructional Design and Assessment (WIDA) 10
writing classroom 69
writing poems 5
writing poetry 5–6
writing process 36, 55–57, 57, 65; asset-focused peer conferring 60; gather ideas 58; genre 64–68; make time to refine and reflect 60–64; mentor texts 58; model your own process 59; publish and celebrate 64; teacher's role in 57; teach genre-specific mini-lessons 59; time to draft & re-draft 59

YouTube 96, 99, 158; content offerings 110; videos 118
YouTube Shorts 12, 59, 109–112, 114

Zillennial 17
zip-ode poems 12, 43, 58, 98–118, 175
zip-ode shorts *97*, **108–109**; rubric and artist statement **121–123**
Zoom 40, 183

For Product Safety Concerns and Information please contact our EU representative GPSR@taylorandfrancis.com
Taylor & Francis Verlag GmbH, Kaufingerstraße 24, 80331 München, Germany

www.ingramcontent.com/pod-product-compliance
Lightning Source LLC
Chambersburg PA
CBHW062222300426
44115CB00012BA/2183